EARLY ISLAMIC POTTERY

The Faber Monographs on Pottery and Porcelain
edited by W. B. Honey

★

★

OTHER TITLES WILL FOLLOW

A. *Slip-painted bowl. 'Samarkand' type; 10th century. Diam.* 13¾ *in.*
Victoria and Albert Museum

EARLY
ISLAMIC POTTERY

Mesopotamia, Egypt and Persia

by
ARTHUR LANE
of the Victoria and Albert Museum

FABER AND FABER
24 Russell Square
London

*First published in mcmxlvii
by Faber and Faber Limited
24 Russell Square London W.C.1
Printed in Great Britain by
R. MacLehose and Company Limited
The University Press Glasgow*

FOREWORD

The beauty of the medieval pottery of Persia had long been known to a small circle of collectors and specialist students when the great display at Burlington House in 1931 came as a new experience to the public at large. With its splendid colour and its wealth of sensitive drawing it plainly belonged to one of the great creative periods in the history of pottery. It was evidently of great historical importance also, obviously inheriting the traditions of Dynastic Egypt and the Ancient East, with their characteristic fondness for turquoise-coloured glazes. But while many accounts have been written of this Persian work alone, little has been done to show how it belonged to a larger world of Islamic culture, in which potters and other artists moved freely from Court to Court over all the Near and Middle East.

This cultural unity of early Islam is one of the principal themes of Mr. Lane's brilliant introduction to this book. Against the skilfully drawn background of Islamic civilisation, which stands in so marked a contrast with the barbarism of Europe in the same period, he traces the rise and fall of dynasties and the fluctuations of patronage. He writes not only of the wares of Rayy, Kashan and Sultanabad within the limits of modern Persia, but of the earlier wares of Mesopotamia— of Bagdad and Samarra, and of the superb pottery known as Samarkand ware, made in Transoxiana in Central Asia. He discusses too the beautiful wares of medieval Egypt, many of them known to us, alas, only by fragments found in the rubbish heaps of Old Cairo. The best of these last date from the time of the art-loving Fatimid Dynasty, whose fall in 1171 drove many gifted Egyptian craftsmen to take refuge and service at the Courts of North-West Mesopotamia; there the famous Rakka wares were made thenceforward. Mr. Lane's survey ends with the thirteenth century, when the establishment of the Mongol Empire throughout Asia brought a new wave of influence from China and began a new epoch. The later Persian and other Islamic pottery will be the subject of a separate volume in this series.

The wares thus introduced form in the hundred plates that follow an astonishing sequence of painted and incised designs of the greatest beauty, variety and interest, including many types now for the first time brought together in a single volume.

W. B. H.

ACKNOWLEDGEMENT

The author wishes to express his gratitude to the authorities of the museums named in the plate-captions for photographs and permission to use them. Especial thanks are due to the Victoria and Albert Museum and the Metropolitan Museum, New York. Sir Alan Barlow and Mr. Tomas Harris have kindly made certain pieces available for photography, and the Oxford University Press has given permission to reproduce photographs from *A Survey of Persian Art*. Some of the pieces described as in the possession of private collectors may since have changed hands, and it is regretted that circumstances have prevented the author from learning their present ownership.

CONTENTS

ILLUSTRATIONS

COLOUR PLATES

MONOCHROME PLATES
after page 52

xi

1

THE ISLAMIC SCENE

Islam was first a religion: it expanded as a militant Arab state, and at length mellowed into a civilization shared by all the territories conquered in its name. When Muhammad died in A.D. 632 his unrealized ambition had been to unite the tribes of Arabia into a nation acknowledging him as its religious and secular head. He cannot have foreseen that in little more than a century the Arab state would become a world power greater in extent than the Roman Empire had ever been, stretching east beyond the Oxus and the Indus, and west through North Africa and Spain to the shores of the Atlantic. The Persian Empire of the Sassanian kings had been absorbed; and the Roman Emperor ruling in Byzantium had been stripped of his provinces all round the eastern and southern coasts of the Mediterranean.

Over this vast territory the Caliphs, or Successors of the Prophet, theoretically wielded supreme religious and secular authority. In actual fact centuries were to pass before the Islamic faith claimed a majority of adherents among the conquered peoples. Meanwhile other religions were tolerated unless they acted as a focus of political unrest. Unbelievers were excluded from administrative posts and paid taxes from which Muslims were exempt; but once they chose to accept Islam they entered a brotherhood that recognized no barriers of race. The shared duty of pilgrimage to Mecca created confidence between peoples of widely different origin; and Arabic, the language of the Koran, became as much a *lingua franca* as Latin in Mediaeval Christendom. From religion the Islamic civilization drew the strength that enabled it to survive all the political storms and invasions that racked the Asiatic continent.

The political authority of the Caliphs commanded less respect than their position as religious figureheads, and the racial ascendancy of the Arabs lasted no longer than the Caliphate of the Umayyad family (A.D. 661–750). During this time the capital was at Damascus, in a former Roman province, and with no urban culture of its own the Arab court had perforce adopted a pattern of life similar to that of the Roman Levant. But in 750 the Umayyads were overthrown by another Arab family, the Abbasids, whose decision to remove the capital eastwards to the new city of Baghdad on the Tigris opened a new epoch. Cultural ties with the Mediterranean were now loosened,

A   1

and Islam became primarily an Asiatic civilization. Persian influence prevailed in what has been aptly called the 'Renaissance of Islam'—the century A.D. 750–850 during which the outstanding figure was Harun al-Rashid, the contemporary of Charlemagne. The Abbasid line held the Caliphate for five centuries. But in that time the political unity of their empire steadily disintegrated. The last survivor of the Ummayads had escaped to Spain and set up a rival Caliphate at Cordova, while local dynasties, owing only nominal allegiance to the Abbasids, established themselves in Egypt and Persia. Moreover, vigorous new races began to invade Asia from the east, as the Arabs had once done from the west, and in the eleventh century Saljuq Turks from beyond the Caspian Sea took over from the Caliph the temporal authority that he had been unable to maintain. The Saljuqs, who were early converts to Islam, once more consolidated the empire and revived its prosperity. But the next wave of invaders from the east were of a very different stamp; the Mongols in the thirteenth century destroyed the Abbasid Caliphs and millions of their subjects before they in turn embraced Islam, and under its influence themselves set about reconstructing the civilization they had almost ruined. This happened at the end of the thirteenth century, the limit proposed for the material discussed in this book.

The progress of Islamic art was inseparably linked with the fortunes of these contending dynasties. By inviting or compelling craftsmen of all nations to come and work for them in Syria, the Umayyad Caliphs set an example followed by all later powers. Baghdad, Samarkand and Cairo in turn became focal points of art and learning, and as one power waned, the craftsmen scattered to mend their fortunes—perhaps with various minor princes, perhaps at the court of a rising dynasty, which thus at one stroke inherited an artistic tradition that had matured elsewhere. This mobility of craftsmen largely explains the surprising uniformity of style throughout the Islamic countries at a given date. But the transport of works of art themselves over great distances also helped to spread styles and techniques—and incidentally to aggravate the problems of the art-historian who hopes to learn where particular things were made.

The study of Islamic pottery still remains in a highly speculative stage. In eastern Islam the decorative tilework used in architecture is the only form of mediaeval pottery that has in any quantity survived above ground. Even so the tiles have often been torn from their setting by dealers, to be dispersed among western collections as incomplete units without their context or origin being known. Pottery vessels began to reach the western market in the 1880's. They had been excavated from rubbish-pits on the sites of ruined cities such as Rayy in Persia or Rakka in Northern Mesopotamia, but dealers' statements as to the provenance of individual pieces were (and are still) seldom to be trusted. Very few pots are entire; most have been pieced together from fragments, and the glaze and painting have lost their brilliance through decay. Yet decay itself sometimes brings compensation, in an attractive patina or iridescence like that so well known on Roman glass. The art of 'restoration' reaches its height on early Islamic pottery; at workshops mainly in Paris missing fragments are replaced by pieces from other vessels or made up in plaster, and the whole so skilfully over-painted as to baffle the most expert eye. Genuine pots are often re-decorated or given fraudulent inscriptions, and in this largely unknown field impossible forgeries have for a time gained credence. Fortunately during the last forty years scientific excavations have been carried out on Islamic sites by trained archaeologists— French, German, and now more particularly American. It is regrettable that British learning, with its fine record in other branches of Islamic study, has so far given little support to its pioneers in Islamic art and archaeology. By these excavations our knowledge of early pottery has been greatly increased; but few kiln-sites have been found, and as the Muslims did not bury vessels with their dead, there are no tomb-groups of pottery and associated objects such as have helped elucidate the history of ceramics in China.

Useful pottery of an unpretentious kind was naturally made everywhere in Islam throughout the seven centuries reviewed in this book. But our main interest must be for the finer wares. As already suggested, their development took place in the historical framework of rival or succeeding dynasties, and, like the potters, we shall have to transfer our attention from one country to another as the story unfolds. Spain and North Africa need not be considered here, as so little of their early pottery is known. Apart from historical events, we must also bear in mind the immense artistic prestige enjoyed in Islam during the early Middle Ages by China. Chinese stoneware and porcelain reached the Near East as early as A.D. 800, and the interest it then aroused seems to have created favourable conditions of patronage without which the Islamic potters might never have embarked on their adventurous course. A second wave of Chinese influence arrived in the twelfth century, and a third in the fifteenth—though the last lies outside our present scope. Imported wares of the T'ang, Sung, and Ming dynasties each at one point rekindled the inspiration of the Islamic potters, and started a new epoch of development. But on the first two occasions at any rate the effect was mainly a technical one; a desire to imitate the appearance of white porcelain led to the adoption in the ninth century of a white surface glaze, and in the twelfth of a white material for the body of the pottery itself. The shapes, ornament and colours associated with these materials were of the Islamic potters' own choice, and represent one of the highest achievements in ceramic history.

2

THE UMAYYAD CALIPHS (A.D. 661-750): THE SOURCES OF ISLAMIC ORNAMENT: AND EARLIER CONTRIBUTIONS TO THE POTTER'S TECHNIQUE

It may be said at once that before the ninth century Islamic pottery was of almost negligible interest. But Umayyad art was important, for the repertoire of ornament it gathered together was the parent of most later Islamic decoration, including that on pottery. Artists were called from east and west to decorate the mosques of Damascus and Jerusalem, and the palaces or hunting-lodges on the edge of the desert such as Mshatta and Kuseir Amra. The western element predominated. Following the late Greco-Roman manner current in Syria, it showed a love of naturalistic animal figures, classical urns, and the coiling vine or ivy.

But in contrast to this Mediterranean, naturalistic style, there was another inherited from the ancient east of Assyria and Babylon. With a superficial veneer of Greco-Roman forms, it had been current in Mesopotamia and Persia under the Parthian (249 B.C.–A.D. 226) and Sassanian (A.D. 226–641) Empires before the Arab conquest. It was a formal art of repeating symmetrical patterns, abstract in tendency, whose favourite motives were the fantastic 'sacred tree', the palmette complete or split in half, the rosette, stepped battlements, and the paired wings used by Sassanian kings as a symbol of royalty.

Islamic artists gradually fused these two styles together, ever preferring the formal to the natural. The vine, for example, was first trained into irregular loops, each containing a leaf and a grape-bunch, sometimes one superimposed on another; then it grew pine-cones and a medley of elongated leaves not its own; at a later phase, especially in the eleventh and twelfth centuries, it grew fantastic blooms that distantly resemble a palmette. The spiral-motive so common as a background on Islamic pottery only betrays its origin as a vine by its habit of growth and the little coiled tendrils that spring at intervals along its stem (1).

(1) *Plates* 22B, 27A, 33B, 34A, 41B, 53C.

Though Islamic art soon discarded the Sassanian full palmette, it made much use of the half-palmette; we find this constantly on pottery of the Abbasid period (1). But the half-palmette, like the vine, degenerated by losing its middle lobe; it thus assumed the 'split leaf' form that we instinctively associate with the word 'arabesque' (2). Moreover, instead of allowing each half-palmette its anchorage on the parent stem, Islamic artists conceived the idea of drawing further stems from the point or lobe of the half-palmette itself—a device that allowed unlimited expansion in any direction (3). If we add that Islamic art felt free to break out of the rectangles, circles and friezes that frame almost all classical decoration(4), and indulge in 'all-over' patterns indefinitely repeated(5); that a natural bent for mathematics found pleasure in the most vertiginous geometrical forms(6)—then we can appreciate the resources of Islamic craftsmen for modulating a design over a surface as awkwardly shaped, for example, as that of a pot.

And in the use of writing as decoration Islamic art stands alone. Neither the Greek nor the Latin alphabets have ever so inspired artists with their visual beauty—save perhaps in an illuminated initial or an interwoven monogram. The Chinese value calligraphy as highly as the Moslems; but Chinese writing is a cadent distillation of which only single characters can be scattered among other ornament. Islamic script is powerful both in monogram and continuity. Its imperious leftward advance binds a design together more strongly and subtly than any repetitive frieze, and the letters themselves can be most variously elaborated without sacrificing clarity. If we forgo pedantic accuracy, the Islamic scripts may be conveniently classed in two groups: the angular *Cufic*, which recalls its origin in stone-carving, and the rounded *neskhi*, suggesting the cursive pen. *Cufic* is the older form, but was retained after *neskhi* became general, both for its religious associations and its good looks. Often both scripts are found together on the same object, the force of one offsetting the blandishment of the other. If the inscription has anything important to say, it is usually a quotation from the Koran. Dedications to named persons, signatures of artists, and dates are comparatively rare on pottery, but wishes for blessing and prosperity to the (anonymous) owner abound. As will be mentioned later, only in Persia do the inscriptions aspire to literary content.

Too much stress has been laid on the Moslem injunction against representing living creatures in art. This is not clearly formulated in

(1) *Plates* 5B, 8, 12B, 25A; (2) *Plates* 48, 72A; (3) *Plates* 38B, 54C, 72A; (4) *Plates* 51A, 54C; (5) *Plates* 16, 18B, 77A, 80A, 90, 91; (6) *Plates* 29A, 30B, 73A.

the Koran, but only in the *Hadīth* or Traditions of the Prophet. It represents a puritan strain found also in Christianity, and if it succeeded in banishing images and paintings from the mosque, it rarely applied to the palaces where Caliph and Emir spent profaner hours. At all dates from the seventh century onwards Islamic artists portrayed human and animal figures in every medium, whenever they had the necessary skill. It must be admitted that they lacked the plastic sense that had become second nature to the Greco-Roman civilization. But in painting, whether on walls, in books, or on pottery, they developed an admirable formula for representing men and animals, aiming at linear rhythm in one or two planes rather than at anatomical or spatial realism. Figures painted on pottery very seldom stand on a 'ground line': they hover, as it were, in the space bounded by the limits of the vessel, to which their poise is judiciously related (1). We must note how deep-rooted was the Near Eastern instinct for two types of composition; the heraldic apposition of two figures on either side of a central tree or similar motive(2), and the processional arrangement of figures in a frieze(3). In abstract design strict symmetry is observed; it is rare to find the balanced asymmetry that is so characteristic of Far Eastern Art (4).

If the ornament of later Islamic art was implicit in work of Umayyad date, so also were certain of the techniques later so brilliantly exploited by the potters. But the Umayyad court itself had no appreciation of pottery, which was relegated to humble service in kitchen and courtyard. In many other epochs of civilization wealthy people have used table-ware of precious metal or glass, and even among the poor, pottery has had to compete with vessels of base metal, wood, or even leather. The Sassanian kings of Persia used some of the finest gold- and silver-ware ever to grace a modern museum, but their servants' pottery remains a disappointing episode in ceramic history. From the twelfth to the fifth centuries B.C. the Assyrians, Babylonians, and Achaemenid kings of Persia had had their palaces and processional ways decorated with wall-facings of brick, modelled with life-size human and animal figures, and covered with polychrome glazes. But by Sassanian times this great Near Eastern tradition had died out.

The techniques from which Islamic pottery was to develop all had their origin in the Mediterranean area, and not in the Asiatic hinterland. The Roman *terra sigillata*, made mainly at Arezzo in Italy and at La Graufesenque in Gaul, had been current from the Atlantic to the Euphrates; it was elaborately moulded with patterns in relief, and

---

(1) *Plates* 12, 28B, 48; contrast the classical manner, *Plate* 2B; (2) *Plates* 42A, 69B, 78B; (3) *Plates* 44, 52B, 53B; (4) *Plate* 33A.

covered with a glossy red surface-colour physically different from true vitreous glaze. This type of colour, used also by the potters of classical Greece, was not adopted in Islam. But Islamic unglazed pottery moulded in relief perhaps represents the survival of *terra sigillata* methods into the Middle Ages. Early in the series of such wares is the small cup and stand shown in Plate 4c, D. Though found at Susa, it was probably made in Syria during Umayyad times. The fine white clay is moulded with an illegible Cufic inscription and with alternate panels of vine and pomegranate stems, in the naturalistic late Greco-Roman manner. Fragments of the same white unglazed ware found at Kish in Mesopotamia are decorated with rosettes and other patterns of Sassanian rather than classical origin.

But the great technical advance of Islamic potters over their Greek and Roman predecessors lay in their use of true glassy glazes combined with decoration in relief or painted. And here Egypt seems to have been the ever-fertile mother of inventions, which were preserved unseen through the centuries until the time came for their wider use. As early as the fourth millennium B.C. the Egyptians were using a true glassy glaze composed of powdered sand, quartz or crystal, with an alkaline flux such as potash or soda. This alkaline glaze could be stained many colours by the addition of metallic oxides, and being transparent, could be applied over painted decoration. The bowl shown in Plate 2A is a typical piece of the fifteenth century B.C., with a turquoise glaze over black painting. In Roman times Egyptian potters adopted the classical vase-forms, and made interesting experiments where the painting itself was carried out in coloured alkaline glazes. An example is shown on Plate 2B. The Egyptian alkaline glaze had the peculiarity of not adhering properly to the vessel unless the clay body material contained an admixture of the same sandy and alkaline elements as were used to make the glaze itself.

Perhaps owing to the difficulty of finding the right materials, alkaline glazes were not adopted in Roman Europe. But a blue-green, yellow, or brown alkaline glaze, presumably derived from Egypt, was widely used in the Syrian-Mesopotamian area in Roman times, both by Roman subjects and by those of the Parthian Empire (249 B.C.–A.D. 226), the eastern enemy of Rome before the rise of the Sassanian kings. The so-called 'Parthian' pottery commonly appeared in classical shapes (1), but there was a progressive decline from classical elegance towards squat and uncouth forms. The body-material was coarse and sandy, the glaze extremely thick. Relief-decoration of masks or figures was consequently rare, except on the slipper-shaped coffins used for a

---

(1) *Plate* 1.

brief period by the Parthians in Mesopotamia. On pots, rivet-shaped bosses or random slicing were more usual forms of ornament. Very little 'Parthian' glazed ware has been found in territories further east than Mesopotamia. The same blue-green 'Parthian' glaze was used through Sassanian times (A.D. 226–641) well into the Islamic period, often on coarse pottery with a characteristic decoration of chip-carved triangular nicks. A few Sassanian glazed vessels in animal or human form are known, but the most successful pieces were the large storage jars that have ever been a standard furnishing in the Near East (1).

It is a rather surprising fact that when Islamic pottery began its full career in Mesopotamia during the ninth century, the alkaline glazes still being used in Syria and Egypt were altogether discarded in favour of glazes fluxed with lead. As a result, the development of free painting under the glaze was postponed for three centuries, for lead-glaze is so fluid in the kiln as to smudge any painting not carried out in thick and rather intractable earthy pigments. But as we shall see, the Ancient Egyptian alkaline glaze and the artificially composed body-material associated with it were rediscovered and improved in the twelfth century, and thereafter became the standard medium of fine pottery throughout the Near East.

Glaze fluxed with the oxides or sulphide of lead, unlike alkaline glaze, will adhere to any ordinary potter's clay. It was known to the Greco-Roman potters, and sparingly used over a wide area from the third century B.C. onwards. The south-east Mediterranean was its natural home. Potteries in Tarsus, Smyrna, or Alexandria may possibly claim the credit for making small objects of luxury such as the moulded cup in Plate 4A, which dates from the first centuries B.C. or A.D. Its outside is completely covered with green, its inside with rich amber-yellow lead-glaze; spur-marks in the well show that it was fired upside down. The moulded ivy-pattern and the shape are obviously copied from a cup of embossed metal. Isolated fragments from Egypt show that small moulded vessels or lamps with a lead glaze must have been made there continuously until the ninth century, when this kind of ware took on a new life in the hands of Islamic potters both in Egypt and Mesopotamia.

---

(1) *Plate 3.*

3

FIRST CONTACTS WITH CHINA: THE ABBASID SCHOOL OF MESOPOTAMIA IN THE NINTH AND TENTH CENTURIES

It has been suggested that the fertility of ceramic genius in Islam from the ninth century onwards owed much to religious sanction, since the *Traditions* of the Prophet forbade the use of gold and silver vessels, and the Abbasid Caliphs set greater store by religious observance than their Ummayad predecessors. But we have only to read Masudi's approving gossip about the Abbasid court, and in particular his anecdotes of Harun al-Rashid's eccentric and extravagant wife, to appreciate how the dead hand of desert theologians had been forgotten. The historian Maqrizi, moreover, preserves a detailed inventory, obviously made by an eye-witness, of the treasures looted by mutinous soldiery from the Sultan Mustansir's palace in Cairo in A.D. 1062 Gold and silver vessels were there in abundance. The astonishing rise of Islamic pottery in the ninth century was in fact due to the discovery by the court that pottery could be an art worth encouraging; and the revelation came in the form of porcelain and stoneware imported to Baghdad from the Far East.

The approximate date of its first arrival is suggested by a passage from a work written in A.D. 1059 by Muhammad ibn al-Husain (Abu 'l Fadl) Baihaki. He states that 'Alī ibn-Isa, governor of Khurasan, sent as a present to the Caliph Harun al-Rashid 'twenty pieces of Chinese Imperial porcelain (*chini faghfuri*), the like of which had never been seen at a Caliph's court before', in addition to two thousand other pieces of porcelain. * A distinction is here drawn between the common Chinese export-wares and the finer wares made for home consumption —a distinction familiar to all students of Chinese ceramics. From

---

* NOTE: I am deeply indebted to Mr. M. Minovi and Dr. R. B. Serjeant for drawing my attention to this important passage, and for their collating of the Calcutta and Teheran editions of Baihaki to extract the full sense. The passage is on p. 425 of the Teheran (1307H) edition.

the ninth century onwards there are many further references in Arabic literature praising Chinese porcelain, which reached Mesopotamia and Egypt mainly by the sea-route round India, while Persia received it also by direct traffic overland. The 'apricot-coloured', the 'cream-coloured', and the 'mottled' varieties are named in order of preference, and to judge from archaeological finds on early Islamic sites, these seem to be the greenish or brownish celadons from Yüeh Chou (resembling in colour the grey-green Damascus apricot); the creamy-white porcelain; and the green-and-brown-splashed stoneware, all of which were made in the T'ang period (A.D. 618–906). Chinese porcelain and stoneware created a demand for fine pottery that Islamic craftsmen were not slow to exploit, first by imitating the Chinese wares and then by adding elaborations of their own.

*   *   *   *

The ruins of Samarra. Baghdad, the seat of the Caliphs, rival to Byzantium as the greatest city of the mediaeval world, was for long the main centre of art in Abbasid Islam. Its ruins lie unexplored below the modern city. Farther up the Tigris, however, are the remains of SAMARRA, a vast mushroom city and palace built and occupied by the Caliphs between 836 and 883 and thereafter abandoned. Pottery-fragments found here in German excavations before 1914, and by Iraqi archaeologists more recently, are of the greatest interest, not least because they can be precisely dated within the short period of occupation. The finer wares were probably made at Baghdad, not at Samarra itself, though a later historian does record the transfer of potters from Kufa and Basra to Samarra at the time of its founding. Finds of precisely similar pottery on other sites in Mesopotamia, Persia, Syria and Egypt show that in the ninth century a considerable export trade from Baghdad had already begun.

Abbasid unglazed wares. For a newly developed art the range of types found at Samarra is astonishing. But it must be remembered that they represent the collective effort of the most ingenious craftsmen of the Islamic world, who flocked to the Caliph's court from all countries. They show an ordered social hierarchy, beginning at the bottom with the humble *unglazed ware*, stamped, moulded, incised, sometimes painted, and often decked with applied clay ornament of varying complexity. The buff or whitish clay is lightly fired and very porous, for a good practical reason: as moisture seeps through the walls it evaporates from the surface and thereby cools the liquid inside the vessel. When boorish elaborations are absent, ninth century unglazed pottery may share the simple elegance in form of contemporary glass

11

vessels (1). The technique has remained one of basic utility in most Islamic countries until the present day, and later examples on Plates 36, 37 show how its ornament conformed with changing fashions.

Lead-glazed 'sgraffiato' wares. In the next higher rank are the red pottery vessels covered with white slip under a clear yellowish lead glaze, splashed or mottled with copper-green, manganese-purple, and iron-brown (2). In appearance they very closely resemble the mottled Chinese stoneware from which they were at first copied, but Islamic pieces were more often decorated with patterns scratched through the white slip to the underlying clay before the glaze was applied (the so-called *sgraffiato* technique). The scratched patterns, usually based on the half-palmette, are often submerged under spots or splashes of colour that bear little relation to them, and the effect is seldom pleasing. Attempts were also made to paint designs, but the colours were so apt to run in the glaze that the results were only successful if limited to simple spots and stripes (3). T'ang mottled wares and their local imitations have been found in places as far apart as Fostat in Egypt, Samarra, Samarkand and Nishapur in Eastern Persia, where the American Expedition recovered the unusually handsome bowl shown in Plate 6B. In fact, from the ninth to the twelfth century or even later pseudo-Chinese mottled *sgraffiato* wares were made almost everywhere in the lands of the Eastern Caliphate.

Lead-glazed relief-ware. On an earlier page we have noticed a class of late Roman pottery decorated with patterns moulded in relief and covered with coloured lead-glazes (4). This technique survived till Abbasid times in Egypt, where small vessels and lamps moulded with animal- or band-patterns were coloured with green, brown, and purple glazes, all three colours being sometimes found side by side (5). A condiment-dish is inscribed 'the work of Abu Nasr of Basra, in Egypt' (6), and a small lobed cup (7) bears in Arabic the name 'Husein'. It appears probable that in the ninth century Egyptian potters introduced the manufacture of this ware to Mesopotamia, for somewhat similar pieces have been found at Samarra. But in the Mesopotamian branch of this interesting family the style of ornament changed; the Hellenistic-looking birds and animals were replaced by Cufic inscriptions, interlacing bands, half-palmettes, arcades, and other motives with a strong Sassanian flavour (8). Besides the opposing Greco-Roman and Sassanian styles, yet a third element appears in the design of glazed relief-wares made in both Mesopotamia and Egypt— that of the green-glazed, lobed bowls of T'ang stoneware with moulded

---

(1) *Plates* 6A, 7A; (2) *Plates* 6B, 7B; (3) *Plate* 7B; (4) See p. 9 and *Plate* 4A; (5) *Plate* 5A; (6) *Plate* 4E; (7) *Plate* 4B; (8) *Plate* 5B.

reliefs, which have been discovered in Egypt and at Samarra. Plate 4F shows a Mesopotamian copy of one of these; there is an Egyptian imitation in the Eton College Museum. The Mesopotamian relief-ware differs from the Egyptian both in its finer body-material and in its colour-scheme. There are no more polychrome effects. Instead, on the finer Mesopotamian pieces, a striking innovation appeared. After the first firing, the glaze was coated with a metallic pigment which, fired once again, came out with the glistening appearance of yellow gold. This was the first experiment in the 'lustre' technique that was to absorb the attention of Islamic potters for centuries to come. Sometimes these primitive 'lustre' wares have large Cufic inscriptions picked out in green glaze.

Tin-glazed painted wares. As already related (p. 11), Arab authors mention three types of Chinese wares. We have discussed the Islamic imitations of the 'mottled' T'ang stoneware (p. 12); and if by 'apricot-coloured' ware we are to understand the Yüeh-type celadons found at Samarra and in Egypt, it may be said that the Islamic potters do not appear to have imitated these much before the twelfth century (p. 23). But imitations of the 'cream-coloured' T'ang porcelain have been found at Samarra together with the genuine article, which reached the Near East mainly in the form of lobed dishes or bowls. It was impossible to reproduce the beautiful surface texture of these by using an ordinary clear lead-glaze over a white slip, and the Mesopotamian potters there-fore hit on a device used long before them by the Egyptians. Tin-oxide was mixed with a modified form of lead-glaze, which by the suspended particles was rendered perfectly opaque and white. When applied to a well-purified yellow or pinkish clay, this glaze achieved a most deceptive similarity to the T'ang porcelain. But fortunately the Baghdad potters did not rest content as imitators. They were tempted to paint on the fine white surface, using cobalt-blue, copper-green, manganese-purple, and sometimes antimony-yellow. Paint and glaze were fixed in a single firing. The designs (1) are a little timid in com-parison with those of the 'Samarkand' wares, and the inscriptions lack force, but to Western eyes they have a candid simplicity not often found in later Islamic ornament. The soft absorption of the cobalt into the glaze in the Teheran bowl (2), is particularly agreeable, like ink on snow. Pseudo-Chinese 'splash' effects, more appropriate to the lead-glazed wares, are often found here also (3). Local varieties of this ware were made in Egypt and Syria, but these lack the blue colour and are painted in green and purple or black on a coarser 'candle-grease' glaze. Another kind is found in the Samarkand area, where green

---

(1) *Plates* 8, 9; (2) *Plate* 8B; (3) *Plate* 9B.

alone is used for the dominant half-palmette and dotted-band designs. Though many pieces of this family have been found at Rayy, Istakhr and elsewhere in western Persia, these are betrayed by the quality of their materials as Mesopotamian imports.

Lustre-painting. The origin of the technique of 'lustre-painting' on pottery has been debated with needless acerbity, but it seems fairly certain that it was first used in Egypt, to decorate glass, sometime in the first two centuries of Islam. The pigment essentially consists of sulphur in various forms compounded with silver-oxide (which on glass or glaze acts as a yellow stain), and with copper-oxide (which apparently contributes the 'lustrous' element). It is probable that other metallic oxides were sometimes present. The manner of application is to mix the pigment with an earthy vehicle such as red or yellow ochre. With this mixture decoration is painted on the surface of a glass or glazed pottery vessel already once fired, using vinegar or wine-lees as a medium. The vessel is then lightly fired for a second time in a reducing kiln (that is, with a minimum of air, plenty of smoke, and no clear flame); it is subsequently removed from the kiln and the adhering ochre gently rubbed away. If all has gone well the metallic elements will have been deposited on the surface of the glaze in a glittering film not perceptible to the touch. Excessive heat or flame burns away the pigment altogether, leaving only the ochre vehicle. The copper is always more volatile than the silver, which is sometimes left behind as a yellow stain without 'lustrous' effect. A thick deposit of pigment may have the appearance of solid copper or greenish gold, and a thinner, transparent film will be shot with the rainbow effects found in mother-of-pearl. It is a hazardous technique, and irregularities in application or firing of the pigment may result in much unevenness of tone on the finished vessel.

Mesopotamian lustre-painted wares. Lustre-painted glass was found at Samarra, though less abundantly than in Egypt; and, as already stated (p. 13), a uniform coat of lustrous pigment was successfully applied to lead-glazed pottery in Mesopotamia during the Samarra period (836–883). But these small pottery imitations of gold objects failed to satisfy once the potters had found in the fine tin-glazed ware a suitable field for painted decoration. The same factories, probably located in or near Baghdad, produced both the blue, green and purple-painted wares (p. 13) and those with lustre-painting. Sometimes, indeed, we find a fore-taste of a common later practice—pieces on which part of the design, say an inscription, has been painted in blue before the first firing, to set off the lustre decoration added in the second stage. It is not alto-gether surprising that in the opening phase of its employment the 'lustre' appears with a great variety of colours, which are deliberately contrasted on a single vessel—in fact, the very designs are often sub-ordinated to the aim of juxtaposing dashes, spots, or squares of different tones. The potters were clearly experimenting with different combinations and proportions of metallic ingredients in their pigment. Most striking is a rich ruby red, developed from copper, but this seems to have been an accidental product of over-firing in which the copper escaped from the painted pattern in the form of a mist over the adjoining areas of white glaze. Many shades of brown and yellow are found, and occasionally red and black. Not all these colours contained the 'lustre' element, which was sometimes applied over them in spots or in an even film. About A.D. 860 a bichrome palette of brown and yellow was regularly adopted, and soon after the evacuation of Samarra in 883 the colour-scheme was further simplified to become a greenish- or brownish-yellow monochrome. Though from the ninth century lustre-painting long continued as the technique most valued by Islamic potters, hardly ever did they again deliberately combine different lustre colours on a single pot. The reason was no doubt an economic one, for the polychrome effects were more laborious to prepare and less certain of success.

The shapes of the Mesopotamian tin-glazed ware, whether painted in 'blue and green' or lustre, were often closely imitated from Chinese models. Thus the spouted ewer with moulded palmette handles is more familiar in T'ang stoneware (1). So are the shallow bowls with outcurved rim and shallow foot-rings, easily stacked for export; and the flat-rimmed dishes, sometimes flat beneath, sometimes standing on knobbed feet. More Islamic in feeling are the straight-sided beakers and jars with multiple handles (2). As for ornament, the ninth century polychrome lustre-ware presents in disordered confusion, barely to be recognized, the old Sassanian wing-motives (3), half-palmettes (4), random foliage, and meaningless herring-bones, spots and squares. The designs have little formal basis; they are only a medium through which the radiance of metallic lustre and white glaze can flatter the eye. In the palace at Samarra were found some square wall-tiles, painted very skilfully in polychrome with cocks in wreaths, after the best Sassanian manner. But with this sole exception, not an animal figure is to be seen on the lustred Samarra fragments, nor on the bichrome lustred tiles still embedded in the walls of the Great Mosque at Kairawan in Tunisia—whither they had been sent, accompanied by a Baghdad potter, about the year 862. It was as though the classical tradition, still capable of producing the big fresco-paintings of men and women in the palace at Samarra, had completely died out in minor art

---

(1) *Plate* 11A; (2) *Plate* 10B; (3) *Plate* 10A; (4) *Plate* 11A, B.

at the Caliph's court. When living forms reappear on the mono-chrome lustre-ware, about the turn of the ninth-tenth century, they are childish *incunabula*, the mental symbols rather than the recorded observations of life (1). The animals never become vertebrate: the humans are rather frightening grotesques—always with faces in front view. We may note the new convention of 'contour-panels', dotted backgrounds shaped to fit the figure. This later became a common-place of design throughout Islam (2); in the fifteenth century it passed from the 'Moresque' pottery of Spain to the painted *maiolica* of Italy. The monochrome lustre-ware of Baghdad was exported to places remote as Samarkand, Brahminabad in Sind, Egypt, and even Medina Azzahra in southern Spain. But by the end of the tenth century the manufacture seems to have dwindled to nothing in Mesopotamia, while a vigorous new school of lustre-painting on pottery was rising in Egypt. In Chapter 5 it will be argued that the best potters of Baghdad had moved on to the Fatimid court in Cairo; but first we must consider a school of pottery contemporary with that of Baghdad, that had arisen to the far east of Persia.

---

(1) *Plates* 12, 13; (2) *Plates* 23B, 24, 57B, 77B.

4

PAINTED WARES OF THE SAMARKAND REGION AND PERSIA

In 820 the Caliph appointed Tahir ibn-al-Husayn governor of the lands east of Baghdad, and when Tahir founded a dynasty ruling first from Merv, and later from Nishapur in Khurasan province, eastern Persia and the territory beyond the River Oxus became for political purposes largely independent of the central government in Baghdad. The most distinguished among successive dynasties here was that of the Persian Samanids (874–999), who resided beyond the Oxus with Bukhara as their capital and SAMARKAND their chief city. Their court sponsored a brilliant revival of literature in the Persian language, as opposed to the Arabic which had been the universal vehicle of culture since the Conquest. More important for our purpose, there arose in the Samarkand area a vigorous school of potters whose methods were essentially different from those currently practised at Baghdad.

The early pottery of this region was unglazed, and at present there is no reason to think that anything finer was produced until Samanid times (874 onwards). Chinese wares have been found near Samarkand, and imitations of the 'mottled' Chinese stoneware made locally are hardly to be distinguished from those of Mesopotamia (p. 12). We must assume that the use of lead-glaze was learnt from the West. But the Samarkand potters made the important discovery that painted decoration, normally so apt to 'run' if the fluid lead-glaze were applied over it, would stay fixed if the metallic colouring agents were mixed with a paste of fine clay slip. Their best wares were finely potted in a red or pink clay which was usually entirely covered with a coat of 'slip' as a ground for the painting. White was the commonest ground-colour, but we also find a vivid tomato-red and purplish-black. The same colours were used in painting, and in addition to them various shades of brown and a peculiarly attractive soft yellowish green. Blue never appeared, but in one rare type a transparent glaze stained green was applied over white slip designs painted directly on to the clay. The slip pigments were so thick that edges and inner details of the design often had to be tidied up with a knife or stick. Bowls with straight or convex sides and flat-rimmed dishes were the commonest shapes, but small jugs, *albarello*-shaped jars, and lamps, are also found. The bases are flat, with a slight recess underneath.

EARLY ISLAMIC POTTERY

It seems that the most sophisticated kind of decoration was also the earliest. Our Plates 14, 15 show some of the bowls and dishes painted in brownish or purplish black, on an ivory-white ground, with various Cufic inscriptions. Their beauty is of the highest intellectual order; they hold the essence of Islam undiluted. The same stark and moving simplicity appears in some other patterns (1). But the half-palmettes of western Abbasid art were also much in evidence; and sometimes, on vessels painted with brown or greenish yellow, we are aware that the potters were trying to imitate both the designs and colours of the Mesopotamian lustre-ware which is shown by fragments from Afrasiyab to have been imported in the ninth and tenth centuries (2). One rare variety of 'Samarkand' pottery has a dark yellow-brown glaze and decoration painted *over* it in opaque white slip, which must have been fixed in a second firing (3); here too the birds in dotted 'contour panels' are strongly reminiscent of the figures on tenth-century Mesopotamian lustre-ware (4).

Human forms never appear in the Samarkand painting, and recognizable animals or birds rather seldom. It seems that in the potters' workshops the western Islamic element represented by the austere bowls with Cufic inscriptions was gradually engulfed by a more barbaric taste. The natives of the region were of Turkish race, and the steppes of Central Asia have been an immemorial home of abstract tendencies in ornament. The Arabic writing and birds on Samarkand pottery became stylized and hardly recognizable; dotted interlaced bands and wild variations on the palmette forms preponderated, as the ware slowly declined in the eleventh century to the status of peasant pottery. But the startling and dramatic brilliance of colour remained admirable to the end (5).

The richest finds of this slip-painted ware were at Nogai Kurgan near Tashkent, and at Afrasiyab near Samarkand, which seems from the number of kiln-wasters discovered to have been one of the main centres of production. But the ware was widely exported; great quantities were found by the American archaeologists at Nishapur in Eastern Persia; and a few pieces at Rayy, Susa, and various places in Baluchistan and Sind.

A rougher provincial ware using the 'Samarkand' technique was made in Persia apparently at SARI, south of the Caspian (6). Its decoration consisted mainly of stylized birds and radiating stalks and flowers ultimately derived from Cufic script.

A more interesting kind of lead-glazed peasant pottery was made

---

(1) *Plates* 16, 18; (2) *Plate* 17B; (3) *Plate* 17A; (4) Compare *Plate* 12; (5) *Colour Plate* A; *Plates* 19, 21A; (6) *Plate* 21B.

during the ninth and tenth centuries in the area of NISHAPUR (1). The buff or grey clay itself often formed the ground for painting in thick slip colours of brown-black, green, carnelian red, and a characteristic bright mustard-yellow. Half-palmette designs (2) suggest connections with western Abbasid art; and the primitive figure of a lady holding a drinking-cup (3) is similar to the figures on tenth-century Baghdad lustre-ware. The background of this piece is blocked in with the striking mustard yellow, and the filling-ornament of birds and rosettes curiously recalls the archaic Rhodian and East-Greek pottery of the seventh and sixth centuries B.C. Other pieces show scattered Arabic inscriptions ('blessings') used in the same anxious but unco-ordinated attempt to appease the horror of empty space.

Peasant pottery painted on a greyish ground in thick yellowish green and white slips, with thinner washes of brown-black and red ochre, was also widely made in Mesopotamia and Syria. As no fragments of this kind were found at Samarra it seems to have been a development of the tenth and eleventh centuries. Half-palmette and interlaced band-ornament was usual on these undistinguished lead-glazed wares, which fall far short of the Samarkand pottery in their attempts to solve the problem of underglaze painting.

It may be added that rough pottery found in the FAYUM in Egypt also shows painting in thick yellow, green and purple colours that themselves contain glaze material, so that no overcoat of lead-glaze was necessary. The designs of simple radiating bands and stripes have little interest.

---

(1) *Plate* 20; (2) *Plate* 20B; (3) *Plate* 20A.

5

EGYPTIAN LUSTRE-PAINTED AND CARVED POTTERY OF THE FATIMID PERIOD (969-1171)

In Eastern Persia the rise of local dynasties virtually independent of Baghdad had created favourable conditions for the 'Samarkand' school of potters. But this school remained somewhat apart from the main development of the craft in Islam. When Egypt in turn broke away from the Caliph's power, it too fostered a notable school of potters; and in this case the potters carried on traditions that had been developed at Baghdad. We could reasonably explain the decline of the Baghdad school in the tenth century, if we assumed that its potters migrated with their secrets to Cairo. In style and technique the Egyptian wares afford strong circumstantial evidence of this, though definite proof may never be forthcoming.

Ahmad ibn-Tulun was sent to Egypt as lieutenant to its governor in 868, and he there established for himself and his descendants a quasi-independent state that also included Syria. For a brief interval after 905 the Caliph's authority was restored, only to be lost to a second ephemeral family of usurpers; finally, both Egypt and Syria were annexed in 969 by a power that had during the previous half-century established control over the whole of North-West Africa. This was the self-styled Fatimid family, which claimed descent from the Prophet's daughter Fatima, but was probably of Persian origin. It followed the dissenting Shia sect of Islam and assumed religious as well as political independence on the Caliphate. The dynasty ruled from Cairo for two centuries (969–1171), and in that time the mainstream of Islamic art passed on from Baghdad to Egypt.

Fatimid lustre-wares. Most Fatimid pottery, and there is plenty of it, has been found in fragments in the rubbish-heaps of FOSTAT—the suburb abandoned when Al-Muizz, the first Fatimid ruler, founded New Cairo close by. This site remained a dumping-ground for many centuries, and the finds also include a great number of fragments of Chinese, Persian, Spanish, Italian and other imported wares. The classification and dating of the fragments rests almost entirely on the internal evidence of style and technique, though kiln-wasters prove beyond doubt that some types were of local make. It is comparatively easy to pick out the imported Mesopotamian lustre-wares, first those of the 'primitive' lead-glazed type (p. 13 and Plate 5B), then those of the tin-glazed polychrome 'Samarra' kind and its tenth century monochrome successor. A somewhat doubtful reference in Maqrizi (see p. 10 above) suggests that Baghdad glazed pottery, along with gold-lustred and 'plain' pottery of presumably local origin, was still counted among the treasures of the Fatimid ruler al-Mustansir dispersed in 1062. But the point at which lustre-painting on pottery began in Egypt cannot be determined by literary or historical records. There are no experimental 'primitives', and with style our only guide we must see the earliest Fatimid pieces as a continuation from the stage reached at Baghdad about the middle of the tenth century.

It should be said at once that the body-materials used in Egypt differed completely from the finely sifted, compact pink or yellowish Baghdad clay. Though they varied a good deal according to the quality of the vessel, and might burn red or greyish yellow, they were as a rule comparatively sandy and coarse. The potting was thus apt to be clumsy, and the shapes lacked that refinement in which the Baghdad potters so carefully followed the Chinese. The Egyptian shapes were for the most part uninteresting—convex or straight-sided bowls with shallow foot-rings, and sturdy jars like the one in Plate 24. Rarely did nicked or lobed rims betray consciousness of contemporary Chinese wares. The white tin-glaze too, though comparable at its best with that used in Baghdad, was often of poor quality, greyish and pitted. And if for a time the entire outer surface was uniformly glazed (the invariable practice at Baghdad), at a later stage the foot was left naked or only lightly smeared. In the quality and variety of its monochrome tones the Fatimid lustre-pigment excels—we find all shades from pale lemon-yellow to a rich, deep copper.

If we could turn over the bowl painted with an elephant (1) we should find on the back a pattern of circles and dashes almost exactly like that on the Baghdad bowls (2). This, like the half-moon border round the elephant, was a formula transmitted from Baghdad to Egypt, where, with variations, it long remained the potter's stand-by. But written small across one of the circles on the elephant-bowl is a revealing inscription—'The work of [I]brahim . . . in Misr' (3). And even if the lustre-ware factories in Cairo were started by potters who had quitted the sinking ship at Baghdad, bringing their trade secrets with them (there is only circumstantial evidence of this, though it is very strong), Ibrahim must have been a Mediterranean man; there is

---

(1) *Plate* 22A; (2) *Plate* 13B; (3) Misr, an alternative name for old Cairo or Fostat.

real observation in his painting, the humps and bumps and wrinkles are taken from life. Since Alexander, Egypt has been a melting-pot of all cultures, and hence the fascinating diversity of Fatimid art; on the one hand, an almost Greek vivaciousness and delight in naturalistic detail (1); on the other, an oriental gift for turning all things, even animals, into a pattern—coldly formal (2), hieratic and pompous (3), or smoothly calligraphic (4). One fragment in the Cairo Museum is painted after a Byzantine model with a figure of Christ, and there are others that recall the paintings in Christian manuscripts. The priest on Plate 26A again reminds us that the local Coptic Christians had retained a popular art of their own since Roman times, and the un-varied repetition of stylized birds and fish (5) is curiously in the tra-dition of early Coptic textiles.

With all these complications it is hard to trace the chronological unfolding of the Fatimid lustre-ware. The elephant-bowl (6) may date from the last quarter of the tenth century; and a fragment (7) bears a dedication to Al-Hakim (ruled 996–1021). The same rather strongly stylized manner, with roundels containing animals either in silhouette or reserved on a dark ground, is found on a series of fragments, some of which bear the potter's name 'Muslim' written inside the base-ring. The unsigned bowls in our Plates 23, 25B are close to this group, which may be tentatively assigned to the first half of the eleventh century: a similar feeling is shown in a number of carved wooden panels thought to have been made for the rebuilding of the Fatimid palace in 1048. Later in the eleventh century a more ragged, *sharawadgi* way of handling ornament developed (8).

The most versatile and productive of the several potters who signed their work was *Sa'd* (9). The inner markings scratched through a lustre ground with a blunt point before firing are very characteristic. Bowls painted in his style or one approaching it have been found built into the external walls of churches at several places in Italy, and also in those of the twelfth-century *hôtel-de-ville* at Saint Antonin in South France (10). These were probably brought back as loot or souvenirs from the Crusades, which set out for the East about 1097. Fatimid pottery must at that time have been common in Palestine and Syria—indeed, Ma'arah near Aleppo was the provenance of a small bowl in the Louvre painted with a hare, closely similar to our Plate 28B, but

---

(1) *Plates* 26B, 27B; (2) *Plates* 24, 25; (3) *Plate* 23; (4) *Plates* 26A, 27A, 28B; (5) *Plates* 24, 28A; (6) *Plate* 22A; (7) *Plate* 25A; (8) *Plate* 22B; (9) *Plate* 26A is signed by him, *Plates* 24, 27A, 28B are in his manner; (10) *Plate* 27A was photographed *in situ* at the Church of San Sisto in Pisa.

diversified with the scratching through a lustre ground so characteristic of Sa'd. Both these last-named bowls show a remarkable innovation in technique. The body-material, under the surface discoloration of the exposed shallow foot, is pure white, very compact, and extremely hard; the glaze is not the usual opaque tin-glaze, but a completely transparent alkaline glaze with a wide crackle, applied direct to the body. In the Victoria and Albert Museum is a lustred bowl-fragment which shows the same peculiarities and bears the signature of Sa'd: it has, moreover, bands of cobalt blue painted under the glaze, and the foot-ring is a deep cylinder. The hard white body-material and the alkaline glaze were common property in the wares to be discussed in our Chapters 7 and onwards, the phase in which Persia took over from Egypt the lead in ceramic development. It is probable that the Egyptian potters learnt the technique from Persia—unless, as seems unlikely, it was discovered independently in both countries.

Fatimid carved wares. Lustre-painted ware was of course only one of the Fatimid pottery-types. The unglazed wares will be mentioned in the next chapter (p. 27), and there were many utilitarian peasant-wares covered with spotted or striped tin- and lead-glazes (see pp. 12, 19). Far more important were the vessels with decoration carved or incised in the body and covered with transparent coloured glazes that formed dark pools in the hollows (1). For these the alkaline glaze and white paste body mentioned above were almost always used. Similar carved and incised designs are found on certain pieces also painted in lustre and signed by the potter Sa'd. The designs of animals and spiral foliage with long coiling leaves are often very like those on wares of the same type made in Persia—indeed it is uncertain whether some pieces found at Fostat are not actually Persian imports. The type seems to have developed during the twelfth century on closely parallel lines in both countries, and in Egypt it remained popular till the fourteenth century at least. One fragment, a kiln-waster from Fostat, shows that the Egyptians were keenly alive to new styles from Persia; it is an imitation of the 'lakabi' ware to be discussed on page 55 (2). Details in ornament sometimes recall the imported Chinese celadons of Yüeh Chou and Lung-chüan that, along with other Sung wares, originally suggested the technique of carved underglaze decoration to the Near East.

In 1171 the Fatimid dynasty collapsed. Their treasures were dispersed by their conqueror, Saladin ibn-Ayyub, who, under the title of Sultan, managed in his lifetime to establish a strong state reaching from the Tigris to the Nile. Saladin recognized the spiritual leadership

---

(1) *Plate* 40B; (2) *Plate* 40B, top right.

of the Baghdad Caliphate; and he reclaimed Egypt from the opposing Shia sect of Islam which in Fatimid times had added a religious barrier to the political estrangement between that country and the orthodox centre of the Faith. His lifelong task was to combat the Crusaders in Syria and Palestine, and Damascus rather than Cairo became his headquarters.

If we judge solely by examination of the Fostat fragments, we must conclude that at some point, perhaps in the latter part of the twelfth century, the stream of ceramic development wavered violently before turning off into a new course. It is reasonable to connect this oscillation with the social upheaval accompanying the fall of the Fatimids. The designs on lustre-painted pottery became suddenly impoverished— medallions or triangles containing human faces, wiry-looking animals, or simple leaf patterns, were typical of the decline. Identical motives were painted in manganese-purple, sometimes over a rather poor tin-glaze, sometimes direct on to a hard white body under a transparent alkaline glaze (1). We find bowls either with the tall cylindrical foot previously mentioned, or with a shallow splayed foot. The latter are as a rule thinly potted in a coarse, hard red earthenware. Then the manufacture of lustre-ware, constant in Egypt for the last two centuries, suddenly came to an end. Lustre-painted fragments in a very different post-Fatimid style have been discovered at Fostat, but in such limited numbers as to suggest that they were imports from Syria, where the lustre technique was used at Damascus in the fourteenth century. If we would see how the stored-up experience of the Fatimid potters lived on, we must look farther afield, to North-West Persia.

---

(1) *Plate* 29B.

6

COMMON POTTERY: THE CERAMIC UNDERWORLD OF ISLAM

Persian sgraffiato wares. The painted wares of Transoxiana (p. 17) were Persia's great contribution to Islamic pottery in the Abbasid age. Elsewhere in Persia the craft seems to have remained at a humbler level until the twelfth century. The painted 'peasant pottery' of Nishapur and Sari has already been described (p.19). Further west were made various local wares, each employing a decorative idiom little affected by the trend of Islamic ornament at the main centres of civilization. The favourite technique was *sgraffiato*, lead-glazed red earthenware with designs engraved through a white slip. We have noticed this procedure in the imitations of Chinese stoneware found at Samarra and other places (1); but in the wilds of Persia many of the *sgraffiato* wares appear to have derived their manner from a different source—namely, engraved metalwork. This should be clear in the laborious decoration of the bowls in Plate 30; it resembles that of early Islamic silver vessels found in South Russia, and has its roots in a surviving Sassanian tradition. Such bowls may date from any time between the tenth and twelfth centuries. Many are said to have been dug up at RAYY near Teheran, but somewhat similar fragments have also been found by Sir Aurel Stein in the area south of Kerman. A more fluent and appropriate handling sometimes appeared—for example, Plate 31A. The glaze was occasionally stained green throughout, or the rim alone might be stained green; but there was no random splashing with green and brown as on the imitations of T'ang stoneware.

Green, brown and purple were used in combination on another small provincial class of *sgraffiato* bowls, most of which were reputedly found at AGHKAND 125 miles S.E. of Tabriz (2). Here the incised lines were used to keep the colours from running outside the pattern, as in a well-known kind of Chinese T'ang stoneware; but the coincidence in technique was probably quite fortuitous, for the designs of animals on a background of stumpy vine-scrolls are purely Islamic and may be compared with those on Fatimid lustre-ware. Two of the existing Aghkand bowls are signed by the potter Bu Talib. Though untouched

(1) *Plates* 6B, 7B, p. 12; (2) *Plate* 34A.
25

by what we shall call the 'Saljuq' ornamental style, they probably date from the thirteenth century—or at earliest, the twelfth.

A third group of Persian *sgraffiato* wares was almost certainly made at AMOL, at the southern end of the Caspian Sea (1). They may be assigned to the thirteenth century and later. Painted green and brown spots and stripes were here combined with scribbled engraving to form disintegrated and often asymmetrical designs, which are sometimes not unpleasing. There is little Islamic character about these bowls, with their angular sides and metallic-looking attachments; only an occasional cursive inscription in Arabic wishing well to the owner.

A fourth group claims more respect (2). There is good evidence that these wares were made at YASTKAND and other remote villages in the GARRUS district of Kurdistan (south-west of the Caspian Sea). The commonest shape was a heavy flat-footed conical bowl with curved-in rim; but there were also straight-sided bowls, flat-rimmed dishes, and ewers of various kinds, sometimes with mouths shaped like animals' heads. A number of large rectangular plaques with holes in the centre have been found. These were apparently set in the walls of the mud-brick houses as a form of architectural revetment. The glaze might be green or colourless, in which case splashes of green were often added. Yellow-brown streaks were often caused by the emanation of iron from the clay, where the white slip had been cut away to form a dark background for the design. It is a forceful technique, and the lugubrious animals that bulk so large in their frame are impressive—though perhaps a little uncouth. So are the Cufic inscriptions (3) and the coiling vine-scrolls, which now take the 'Saljuq' forms later to be discussed. The Garrus *champlévé* wares would seem for the most part to be rustic contemporaries of the fine lustre-painted pottery of Rayy, in the later part of the twelfth and the thirteenth centuries. Dealers have named them *gabri* wares, in the mistaken belief that they were connected with the Zoroastrian fire-worshipping (*Gabri*) inhabitants of pre-Islamic Persia.

Sgraffiato wares of Mesopotamia and Egypt. The *sgraffiato*-wares so far described were no doubt highly prized by their provincial owners. But as in the Abbasid age, so in later times even the more sophisticated communities needed both unglazed and *sgraffiato* pottery for common use. A bowl found near Aleppo, for example (4), echoes the spirit of the painted or lustred Rakka wares at a lower social level; and up and down the Syrian coast the Crusaders were habitually using *sgraffiato* wares of local make (5). It was surely from the Near East that the

_____

(1) *Plates* 32A, 33A; (2) *Plates* 31B, 32B, 33B; (3) *Plate* 31B; (4) *Plate* 35B; (5) *Plate* 35A.

sgraffiato technique extended its hold on Italy, where it was to become in due course a humble companion of the more expensive painted maiolica. In the Egypt of Saladin's Ayyubid successors (1171–1250), and of the Mamluk regime that followed (1250 onwards), the *sgraffiato* ware took a very distinctive form (1). Basins (some very large) with high, narrow, feet and flaring sides are commonest. They often carry the armorial shield of the noble families for whose kitchens they were made. White or brown slips are locally applied to emphasize the patterns, which consist mainly of pious or sycophantic writings in a big *neskhi* script. The glaze is monochrome, yellowish or green. Occasionally we find animal patterns done in white slip on the red clay ground. They are beasts of the lean, prancing kind that has been associated with the transitional phase after the Fatimid *débâcle* (2). Detailed and interesting animal or human figures may appear, though rarely, on these rather tedious Mamluk pots.

Unglazed wares. The unglazed pottery of Abbasid times has already been briefly noticed (p. 11). Commercial diggers have thought this kind of ware unprofitable, so that it is rather poorly represented in Western collections. This is a pity, for the shapes are often good and the decoration shows a keen sense of the manipulative quality of the clay. Small water-jugs or pots were made in separate parts, each formed in a hollow earthenware mould containing countersunk ornament: the parts were then joined horizontally round the bulge and the seam smoothed down (3). Or simple ornaments might be stamped in the unfired surface, which was often subtly dimpled with thumb impressions (4). The walls are usually very thin, and the finely-sifted whitish clay readily takes up any kind of relief-decoration. Water-jugs commonly had filters built into their necks to keep out the flies, and in Egypt especially these were pierced with lace-like patterns of great delicacy (5). Another kind of vessel found in great quantities all over the Near East is the heavy pear-shaped bottle with a small mouth from which the contents can be dispensed drop by drop (6). These are often elaborately decorated with relief-patterns, and sometimes glazed. Teutonic intuition has suggested that they are incendiary bombs, to be hurled full of naphtha or petroleum against military objectives with lighted brands to follow (strong men who have tested them against stone walls say they seldom break). But one found recently at Samarra has an inscription showing that it was meant to contain vintage wine. Otherwise the bottles might be used to sprinkle rose-water or perfume. Big drum-shaped 'pilgrim bottles' seem peculiar to Mesopotamia and

(1) *Plate* 34B. (2) *Plate* 29B; (3) *Plate* 36A, C; (4) *Plates* 36A, B; (5) *Plate* 36D, E; (6) *Plate* 36F.

Syria, and sometimes bear heraldic devices of the Mamluk kind (1). In North Mesopotamia were made some tall water jars with very elaborate modelled decoration forming a screen round their necks (2); the human and animal figures on these bring them into close relationship with the twelfth-thirteenth century painted wares of Rakka (see p. 38).

(1) *Plate* 37A; (2) *Plate* 37B.

7

THE SALJUQ TURKS AND THE NEW EPOCH OF POTTERY IN PERSIA

The twelfth century, like the ninth, was a turning point in the history of Islamic pottery. The successive schools of Baghdad and Cairo had led in the earlier phase, with the vigorous school of Samarkand standing rather apart from them in the east. Now the lead passed to Northern Persia.

The political background for this re-grouping of artistic forces in Islam was the ascendancy of the Saljuq Turks in Asia and the over-throw of the Fatimid dynasty in Egypt. A new and more supple treatment of design appeared in all the arts, including that of the potter; but here once again, as in the ninth century, Chinese porcelain set a standard of technical discipline that had to be mastered before the Islamic potter could go his own way. In the first epoch of Islamic pottery the whiteness of porcelain was counterfeited by a surface glaze laid over comparatively crude earthenware; in the second, the whiteness lay in the artificial composition of the body-material itself.

About the middle of the tenth century, a Turkoman chieftain named Saljuq led his clan westwards from the Khirgiz steppes of Turkestan, and settled in the territory of Bukhara. The Turks became fervent Moslems: they advanced yet further west: and in 1055 Saljuq's descendant, Tughril Beg, entered Baghdad as a conqueror. While respecting the spiritual authority of the Caliph, he brought under his own rule the whole of western Asia with the exception of Syria. After 1071 Asia Minor was captured from the Byzantine Empire, and a branch of the Saljuq tribe was installed with its capital first at Isnik (Nicaea) and later at Konia (Iconium). They called themselves the Saljuqs of Rum (Rome). Needless to say the central authority of the Grand Saljuq gradually weakened as local Turkish dynasties consolidated their power. We have already mentioned one such dynasty—that of Saladin and the Ayyubids (1171–1250), who destroyed the Fatimid house in Egypt. The court of the Grand Saljuq himself did not settle permanently in a single place, and there was therefore no unique concentration of culture of the kind formerly represented by Baghdad and Cairo. Certain towns prospered exceedingly through their position on trade highways, and here arose the potters' kilns.

RAYY, the Rages of *Tobit* 4: 1, lay on the main route across northern Persia. From its ruins five miles south-east of modern Teheran have come enormous quantities of mediaeval pottery. Kiln-wasters show that some of the best wares of the Saljuq period were made there, but the places of manufacture of other types said to have been found at Rayy are still unknown. KASHAN, some 125 miles south of modern Teheran, had a great reputation for its pottery and tiles. Thanks to the discovery of kiln-wasters, and the potters' habit of signing and dating their tiles, the Kashan wares have been reasonably well identified. But later during the thirteenth century the Kashan styles were also practised in the region of the modern SULTANABAD, which lies half-way between Kum and Hamadan. Outside Persia, the great caravan city of RAKKA on the Euphrates in Northern Mesopotamia had important potteries. Its ruins are everywhere pitted by the more or less furtive excavations of local peasants, and finds made by more responsible authorities are in the Topkapu Serai Museum at Constantinople. The Rakka wares are easy to distinguish from the Persian wares on technical grounds; but it has been claimed that similar pottery was also made at RUSAFA, no great distance away, and some Rakka types are in style and technique almost identical with those made in CAIRO. These then were the main potting centres of the Saljuq period, as at present known. In view of the general similarity between their products, and the existence of many wares whose home has not been traced, it seems better to discuss and compare the Saljuq wares according to technique, rather than to follow up developments at each place.

The Saljuq ornamental style was a development of something that already existed in Islamic art. The half-palmettes and coiling vine-scrolls so characteristic of earlier Mesopotamian and Egyptian pottery are now quickened into a more nervous, flickering life. The half-palmette loses its central lobe and becomes a split-leaf arabesque, often fantastically elaborated (1); it takes its place on the vine, whose long prehensile leaves strive to clasp any part of the stem within reach (2). Some of the vine-leaves blossom into a complicated flower that somewhat resembles a full palmette (3). Throughout there runs a sinuous, undulating rhythm; the angularity of Cufic script is smothered under foliage, and the rounded *neskhi* writing is obviously considered more sympathetic in an art whose object is to produce a soft and closely woven texture over the whole decorated surface (4). In Persia especially this kind of ornament developed into half-naturalistic plant-

---

(1) *Plates* 48, 54C, 55A, 56B, 80B; (2) *Plates* 39B, 44, 72B; (3) *Plates* 41B, 52C, *Colour Plate* C; (4) *Plates* 42, 57A, 62A, 72A.

forms that are often disposed or balanced with a sensibility that appears quite free of formal rules (1). Figures, human or animal, for a time bulk as large in their frames as they did on early Mesopotamian or Fatimid wares (2), but quite soon they are multiplied till they lose their individual significance and merge on equal terms with other elements of the design (3).

Saljuq ornament began to appear in stucco-work and textiles in the second half of the eleventh century, but the Persian potters, still grappling with technical problems, hardly caught up with the artistic idiom of their age till after the middle of the twelfth century. It is interesting to observe that echoes of the style had reached Egypt before the collapse of the Fatimid dynasty in 1171; it is found both on late Fatimid lustre-painted wares and on carved wares (4).

Chinese porcelain and stoneware were imported into the Near East continuously throughout the Middle Ages, and it seems highly probable that types similar to those found at Samarra, which belong to the T'ang dynasty (618–906), still formed the bulk of the Chinese export wares when At-Ta'alibi was writing, about the beginning of the eleventh century. Both he and his contemporary Al-Beruni (d. 1048) enumerate the three main kinds we have mentioned above (see p. 11). Beruni adds an anecdote of a visit made by him to a merchant friend from Isfahan, who lived at Rayy and owned pots of every kind and shape—all of Chinese porcelain; he also gives a detailed but highly imaginative account of the immense care the Chinese potters devoted to the preparation and maturing of their clay. We are still very ill-informed as to the chronological development of Chinese ceramics during the Sung dynasty (960–1279); but from the evidence of Chinese writers and datable pieces it seems probable that what we recognize as the 'Sung style' did not reach full maturity until the beginning of the twelfth century. It was then that the Kuan and Ju Imperial kilns were founded, and that the Ting wares were at their best. If indeed there was a renaissance in ceramic art in China at this time, it must have led to an improved standard in the wares made for export to the Near East. Fragments of the ivory-white 'Ting' wares, and of the white *ying-ching* porcelain with its faintly bluish glaze, have been found on the trade routes near Aden, at Aidhab on the Red Sea, and at Fostat. Though few finds in Persia have yet been reported, there is the strongest internal evidence that Persian potters imitated these improved Chinese export-wares, whose first arrival in the Near East must have aroused the greatest interest.

---

(1) *Plates* 64B, 84A, 86; (2) *Plates* 52–54; (3) *Plates* 55C, 68, 69; (4) *Plates* 28B, 40B.

Both Ta'alibi and Beruni, writing in the first half of the eleventh century, refer with admiration to the translucency of Chinese porcelain, to its thinness, and to its resonance when struck. None of these qualities were present in the Islamic pottery of those times. They depend on the combination of china clay (kaolin) and china stone (petuntse) as a body-material, and the partial vitrification of these through a very high temperature of firing. We have already mentioned that late in the Fatimid period some Egyptian wares were made of a hard white paste with a transparent alkaline glaze (see p. 23). Precisely the same materials were used in Persia, for pottery which at first obviously attempted to imitate the texture and style of Chinese Ting and *ying-ching* porcelain. As the Persian wares show no Egyptian influence in other ways, and are very much finer, Persia should probably claim the credit for discovering a technique that spread everywhere and completely revolutionized the character of fine Islamic pottery from Saljuq times onwards. The white body is an artificial paste, and we know how it was made. In a Constantinople library there is a most interesting manuscript treatise on the technique of the Saljuq potters written in A.D. 1301 by one Abulqasim of Kashan, who himself belonged to a distinguished Persian family of potters. He describes the preparation of a glass 'frit' from powdered quartz-pebbles and potash melted together in almost equal quantities; this 'frit', powdered and mixed with water, served as the alkaline glaze, with or without added colouring-matter. The body-material consisted of 10 parts powdered quartz to 1 part of the same 'frit' and 1 part white plastic clay. Wares made within the limits of the formula naturally show wide differences of quality, depending on the goodness of local materials and the care spent in their preparation. The great advantage of this technique was that glaze and body, being mainly composed of the same substances, fused inseparably together and could not flake apart in the same way as the lead-fluxed tin-glaze and earthenware body used earlier in Mesopotamia and Egypt. Moreover, the whiteness of the clay made the use of a slip unnecessary; a stained or colourless glaze could be applied over decoration carved, moulded or painted; and the glaze could itself be made opaque by the addition of tin-oxide. The Islamic potters had now in fact re-discovered a technique practised long before by the Egyptians of Dynastic and Roman times, but which had been in abeyance since the ninth century (see p. 8).

B. *Dish with carved ornament and coloured glazes. Persian ('Lakabi' type)
mid-12th century. Diam. 16 in.
Mrs. Tomas Harris Collection*

8

SALJUQ CARVED, MOULDED AND SILHOUETTE-PAINTED POTTERY: TWELFTH-THIRTEENTH CENTURIES

Persian white wares. Plates 38, 39 show some of the Saljuq 'primitives'. Most are said to have been found at Rayy, but they have close affinities in technique with the later wares known to have been made at Kashan. The white paste is exceedingly hard, compact and fine. When the walls of the vessel are thin enough, they are highly translucent. In fact, the material is a 'soft-paste porcelain' rather than earthenware, related in kind to the French *pâte tendre* of the eighteenth century, which was composed in a similar way from glass frit, powdered silica, and white plastic clay. The transparent glaze, laid directly on the paste, is colourless or ivory-tinted; it is full of minute bubbles and subject to deep cracking and pitting in decay. Sometimes the glaze has entirely decayed, unmasking the sharpness of the carving it covered (1).

Many of these white bowls are quite plain, with lobes or nicks in their rims like those common on Chinese stoneware and porcelain. The gadroon ornament on the bowl, Plate 38c, is copied from Chinese *ying-ching* ware; and the wavy rim and general contour of the 'posset-pot', Plate 38A, are strongly reminiscent of a form found in *ying-ching*, Ting, and 'Honan temmoku' wares. On Plate 39D we see what appears to be a conscious imitation of the unglazed lip common to both Ting and *ying-ching* porcelain. Sometimes ornament of Chinese cloud-scroll form appears on the interior of bowls, faintly incised under the glaze like the *an hua*, 'secret', decoration beloved by the Sung potters. But some shapes, such as the beaker (2) are purely Islamic, and the carved or incised ornament quickly develops from a Chinese into an Islamic idiom—at first laboured (3), then more confidently using half-palmette or split-leaf motives (4), and at length full-fledged with *neskhi* inscriptions (5). As if to exaggerate the quality of translucence, the walls are often pierced with little holes that take shape as patterns. These 'windows' are of course filled in by the colourless glaze (6). The

---

(1) *Plate* 38B; (2) *Plates* 39A, B; (3) *Plate* 38B; (4) *Plates* 39B, C; (5) *Plate* 39A; (6) *Plate* 39B.

exquisite refinement and finish of these earliest Saljuq white wares can hardly be over-praised. There is no external evidence for dating them, though the late Fatimid lustre-painted bowl in Plate 29A shares with them the lobed rim inspired by a revived interest in Chinese porcelain. But their obviously experimental character and comparative scarcity suggest that they developed over a fairly short period, starting not earlier than the twelfth century.

Monochrome carved wares. Perhaps about the middle of the twelfth century, the same potters began using glazes stained in various colours. The bowl on Plate 41A is glazed in dull cobalt-blue, and with its compact, clean potting is a delightful object to handle; if the shape and 'sliced' manner of carving are Chinese, the ornament, like that of its companion Plate 41B, is a robust and characteristic example of the mature Saljuq style. Other Persian pieces are glazed in soft purple, yellow, green or brown (1). One group of early carved wares, mainly found at Rayy and probably made there, is rather more clumsily decorated than those so far discussed; the glaze runs into a fine crackle, and the coarser paste is often pinkish in tone (2). Egyptian carved pottery has already been mentioned (3); sadly enough Fostat has yielded practically no complete survivors of this kind, which if anything excels in beauty the Persian ware it so closely resembles. The 'sliced' carving of the twelfth century fairly soon gave way to a procedure that left animal figures, inscriptions and coiling foliage standing in low relief. There are some very splendid Persian water jars, usually with an opaque turquoise or vivid dark blue glaze (4); at Rakka, where the carving was usually rougher, jars with relief carving were either monochrome-glazed or painted in lustre and blue (5). From Rakka, too, come pottery objects of household furniture such as pierced lamps, incense-burners, and small floor-tables on which to stand the drinks (6).

Moulded wares. As has already been shown, Islam had a long tradition of applying relief-ornament to unglazed pottery from moulds, and before the end of the twelfth century vessels were being moulded in the new artificial paste and covered with monochrome glazes. It was a cheaper substitute for carved ware, but less satisfactory. A mould could not produce the sharp edges that so clearly defined the design against the dark pools of glaze that settled in the hollows (7). Pots were often moulded in two vertical halves and the decoration almost obliterated down the seam where they joined. Moulds were commonly used for tile-work with raised decoration, from the thirteenth

---

(1) *Plate* 40A; (2) *Plate* 43; (3) See p. 23 and *Plate* 40B; (4) *Plate* 44; (5) *Plate* 60A; (6) *Plate* 45; (7) *Plate* 42.

century onwards, and also for the rare statuettes and vases in human or animal shape.

Polychrome 'lakabi' carved wares. Plain white carved wares had their vogue in twelfth-century Persia, to be followed by those glazed in rich monochrome colours. A third step in evolution was the attempt to use glazes of different colours side by side in the ornament of a single vessel. The designs were carved in a kind of *cloisonné* manner, with grooved or raised outlines to segregate the coloured glazes in their appropriate areas (1). On open dishes fired face upwards the technique won a precarious success, but on upright jars the colours still tended to run downwards (2). A rich blue, yellow, purple and green were used, in luminous tones graduating from the rich dark pools in the hollows to the thin wash over the raised parts of the carving, where the white body showed through the glaze. The designs of animals and birds have a grand simplicity imposed by the difficulty of the technique. Nothing could be more felicitous than the lively rhythms of the dancer with her drummer and harpist on Colour Plate B; rhythms taken up by the oblique cutting filled with glaze on the dresses and on the hyenas in the foreground. It has been mistakenly suggested that the scene is derived from a Chinese source, but in fact all details, including the head-dress of the dancer, can be paralleled elsewhere in Islamic art of Saljuq times. These polychrome wares, which have been given the nickname *lakabi* (painted), are made of the same extremely fine and hard material as the best white and monochrome carved wares shown in Plates 38, 39, 41. They undoubtedly came from the same factories, perhaps at Kashan. But they were widely exported—pieces have been found in Egypt; and our Plate 40B (top right) shows a kiln-waster from Fostat that bears witness to local imitation. After a short time the *lakabi* technique was given up as too difficult and uncertain in its results. The future lay with painted decoration, though further experiments were necessary before this became a fluent medium.

Persian silhouette-wares. For the alkaline glaze shared with the lead-glaze of an earlier period a tendency to smudge decoration painted under it. At Samarkand in the ninth and tenth centuries the problem had been brilliantly solved by mixing the colours with a thick, opaque clay slip, and much the same procedure was followed in a group of Persian twelfth-century wares (3). But now black alone was used, laid directly on the white paste. Both knife and brush were employed to give the utmost clarity to outlines and inner markings; sometimes the

---

(1) A somewhat similar method had been followed in the lead-glazed Aghkand *sgraffiato* wares—see p. 25 and *Plate* 34A; (2) *Plates* 46, 47; (3) *Plates* 48–51.

design was literally carved through a sombre black ground. Over all was laid a transparent glaze, either ivory-tinted or deep turquoise. The vivacity of the single human figures, such as the devil-dancer in Plate 49A, has invited comparison with the silhouette puppets used in the 'shadow-plays' then, as now, so popular in the Near East; but it seems more likely that the dramatic intensity is inherent in the technique itself. The silhouette wares are thinner in potting than most of the polychrome *lakabi* pieces, and are made of a coarser paste. They may have been made at Rayy. The dishes often have a curious high pedestal foot, which is also occasionally found in Rayy lustre-ware (1), and the wide range of shapes includes many that were to become standard forms in the Saljuq overglaze-painted wares of the late twelfth and thirteenth centuries. A bowl with straight expanding sides and a high, cylindrical foot-ring (2) is perhaps the most characteristic of these. The high foot-ring is not found in the *lakabi* wares, though it appears outside Persia both at Rakka and in the late Fatimid lustre-ware of Egypt.

---

(1) *Plate* 48B; (2) e.g. *Plate* 92B.

C. *Bowl with design cut through black slip under clear turquoise glaze.*
Persian; about 1180. Diam 7⅞ in.
Sir Alan Barlow Collection

9

PERSIAN AND MESOPOTAMIAN
LUSTRE-PAINTED WARES:
TWELFTH-THIRTEENTH CENTURY

The school of Rayy. As already stated, lustre-painting had been the chosen medium of a tremendously vital school of potters in Egypt, which faded out when the Fatimid dynasty collapsed in 1171 (see p. 24). Quantities of lustre-painted pottery have been found at Rayy, and kiln-wasters prove that one large class is of local make (1). Unlike their predecessors, the potters of Saljuq Persia often wrote the date of manufacture on their wares, and the earliest lustre-painted piece so inscribed is a Rayy bottle in the British Museum dated 575 of the Moslem era (A.D. 1179).

The decline and final extinction of lustre-painting in Egypt seems to coincide with its rise in Persia and at Rakka in Northern Mesopotamia. Though no confirmation is to be found in historical records, a plausible suggestion has been made that at this point the Egyptian potters migrated abroad in search of better markets, taking their trade secrets with them. That the lustre technique was a 'secret', maintained in the hands of perhaps a very few families, is apparent from its earlier history. As we have seen (p. 18), the Samarkand potters of the ninth and tenth centuries copied the patterns of imported Mesopotamian lustre-ware but did not know how to copy its technique. And when the manufacture of lustre-ware began to flourish in Egypt, it began to die out in Mesopotamia, its original home. There is at any rate some circumstantial evidence for the later transference of the industry back into Asia.

We find no experimental pieces at Rayy; on its first appearance in Persia the technique is fully mature, and there are definite links in style that suggest the grafting of the Fatimid tradition on to a Persian stock. Compare the Egyptian falconer (2) with the horseman on a Rayy dish (3). Though the latter shows greater sensibility of line, the design is essentially the same. Now compare this rider with the polo-player on the dish beside him (4). The linear calligraphy is here still more fluent, the moon-face a Persian (or more probably Saljuq-

---

(1) *Plates* 52–58; (2) *Plate* 26B; (3) *Figure* 52C; (4) *Plate* 53C.

Turkish) type of beauty. One might suggest that the left-hand dish was painted by an Egyptian, the right-hand one by a Persian: indeed, the second dish in its treatment of foliage rather resembles the lustre-wares of Kashan, whither this particular artist may have moved to help set up a rival school. In the background are the extravagant split-leaf arabesques and tentacle-leaves on a coiling stem, typical of the Saljuq style—though here the fluent brush takes liberties that were impossible in the severe carved and silhouette-wares. Indeed, all Rayy lustre-pottery is painted in a rather sketchy, ragged manner—the manner towards which Fatimid art was developing and which became general in Egypt during the Ayyubid period (1171–1250). We may note the half-moon border, the 'contour panels', and the reserving of figures against a dark background as further links with the Fatimid wares (1). At first the figures are painted big with individual character, as in Egypt, but soon a purely Persian taste reduced them to little repeating motives in an ornamental framework—for example, the Chicago dish dated 587 H/1191 A.D. (2). No doubt this fashion derived from miniature-painting in books, and as the polychrome 'minai' wares were better adapted for such work, the Rayy potters soon lost interest in lustre. Thirteenth-century pieces are often dull and perfunctory (3).

The paste used for the Rayy lustre-ware is hard and rather coarse; it weathers to a pinkish tone where exposed (4). The glaze received a slight admixture of tin-oxide to whiten the ground for painting, yet not sufficient to make it quite opaque. The backs of dishes are almost always covered with a transparent deep blue glaze, and other vessels often have blue glaze under the foot or inside. Sometimes lustre-painting is done on a ground entirely blue, or on one divided into alternate panels of transparent blue and semi-opaque white glazes. It is not irrelevant to note that some late Fatimid lustre-painted ware, including pieces signed by Sa'd, also show blue streaks or panels (see p. 23).

The School of Rakka. The ruins of this great caravan city on the Upper Euphrates have also yielded quantities of locally-made lustre-ware. There is no reason for dating any of it earlier than the presumed dispersion of the Fatimid potters in 1171, and the manufacture probably ended when the Mongols sacked the city in 1259. Carved monochrome Rakka wares have already been mentioned, underglaze painted wares will be (pp. 34, 44); all are made of a white quartz body-material, softer than the Persian and more sugary in texture. As at

---

(1) Compare *Plates* 25B, 27B, 28B, 53, 54; (2) *Plate* 55C; (3) *Plate* 58A; (4) We have noticed similar characteristics in the silhouette wares and in one group of monochrome carved wares—see pp. 36, 34, *Plates* 42A, B; 43.

Rayy, much use is made of a rich blue in combination with the lustre-painting, which always has a very distinctive chocolate-brown tone. The glaze is greenish, transparent, and often thick. It is deplorably apt to decay, concealing the decoration under an opaque iridescent film. Human or animal figure-subjects are rather uncommon: we find them big, as in Fatimid lustre-ware (1), or sometimes deliberately copied from Rayy pottery (2). Most characteristic are the large jars or jugs, often carved in high relief, with very vigorous Saljuq arabesque patterns and *neskhi* inscriptions in 'contour panels' (3). Generally speaking, the Rakka wares tend to be coarser and more carelessly painted than the Persian—we may note the perfunctory scribbles that take the place of Cufic inscriptions in the border. Absence of whitening-matter in the glaze gives them a dingy appearance in comparison with the Rayy and Kashan lustre-wares.

The schools of Kashan and the Sultanabad area. Kashan may have played a leading part in the early development of Saljuq pottery in Persia (see pp. 33, 35), but it earned its great reputation chiefly through the manufacture of wall-tiles painted in lustre, with the frequent addition of relief-modelling and blue glaze to pick out inscriptions. The lustre technique may have been introduced here at a slightly later date than at Rayy, and the style no longer shows vestiges of Fatimid taste. To this day many tile-*mihrabs* have survived above ground. They are quasi-architectural compositions, whose separate parts are often very large, built into the interior of mosques or shrines to indicate the direction towards which worshippers should turn in prayer (4). They were exported far and wide in Persia, where the words *kashi* or *kashani* (of Kashan) have become common names for a tile. Most were made by members of a single family whose signed and dated work ranges from 1215 to 1334, and maintains a remarkable conservatism in style (5).

Other tiles were made in interlocking star- and cross-shapes, to be set as a dado round the walls of mosques, or of secular buildings—in which case they were painted with human or animal figures, surrounded by Persian verses in the moralizing or amorous vein so well known to us through the *Rubaiyat* of Omar Khayyam (6). Designs precisely similar to those on the star-tiles are used to decorate bowls

---

(1) *Plate* 57B; (2) Compare *Plates* 58, 59; (3) *Plates* 57A, 60A; (4) *Plate* 66; (5) Abulqasim of Kashan, who wrote the technical treatise mentioned on p. 32, was a member of this family, and may himself have been a potter. But his book was actually written in 1301 at Tabriz, which had then become the seat of the Mongol court; (6) *Plate* 67.

and other vessels (1). In technical quality the Kashan lustre-ware stands very high. Blue is less commonly added to the glaze than at Rayy; blue and green are, however, sometimes present as pale, even staining over certain areas of the design. The decoration is thoroughly Persian; great beaming moon-faces, each with a halo for beauty rather than saintliness, loom out of a darker background in which bodies, foliage, flying birds, and little spirals are almost indeterminably interwoven. Rayy and Rakka painting looks crudely assertive beside this caressing diminuendo of curves, in which the beautifully inscribed poems round the border have a share. A sample poem may be quoted, from a lustre-painted jug in the Godman Collection dated 669 H/1270 A.D.: '*I am wandering in the desert separated from my love. I write these words on this flask that they may be a remembrance of me in the year of the Hijra 669. Trusting that she of whom I dream ever more, may refresh herself by putting this pitcher to her lips; that she will know my writing and think of me and take pity on my love.*' On the big dish dated 607/1210 (2) Prince Khusrau discovers Shirin bathing, a subject probably taken from the romantic poem written by Nizami some thirty years before. The Kashan painters ever and again repeat the conversation-piece under an awning, beside the garden pool. Only towards the end of the thirteenth century do signs of the tremendous upheaval of the times creep into the idyll, when the picnickers begin to wear Mongol hats, and strange phoenix-birds, dragons and lotus-flowers derived from Chinese art, take their place among the designs (3). Many of these later pieces may have been made in places whither potters had moved from Kashan, such as Sava, the Sultanabad area, and perhaps Nishapur. The Kashan style of lustre-painting survived in Persia even into the fifteenth century.

---

(1) *Plates* 61–64; (2) *Plate* 64C; (3) *Plate* 65C.

10

THE 'MINAI' AND 'LAJVARDINA' PAINTED WARES OF PERSIA: TWELFTH-FOURTEENTH CENTURY

Though the ceramic colours that can be derived from metallic ores and oxides are very numerous, it has always been a problem to reconcile their behaviour in the kiln with that of the glaze. The heat necessary to fuse a glaze on to a vessel tends either to destroy the colour or to affect its stability. Towards the end of the twelfth century Islamic potters frankly recognized that if they wanted polychrome painted effects, two courses were open to them. They could either restrict their palette to the few colours that would withstand the heat necessary to fire and glaze the pot in a single operation; or they could glaze and fire the pot first, and then apply painting in less stable colours that were fixed by firing the pot again at a much lower temperature. The double firing had been practised since the ninth century for painting in lustre. It is therefore surprising that, apart from the poly-chrome lustre-ware of Baghdad (see p. 14), experiments with other 'low-temperature' colours were not made earlier—especially in Egypt under the Fatimids. In fact, such colours were used only by Persian potters, and were never adopted in Syria or Egypt.

There were two ways of using low-temperature colours. In the first, the *haft rang* or 'seven-colour' process described by Abulqasim of Kashan (see p. 39), parts of the design were painted in clear pale blue, purple and green on or under the raw glaze before the pot received its first firing; black outlines and other supplementary colours mixed with a vitreous flux were then added and fixed in one or more further firings at a lower temperature. Conspicuous among the supplementary colours were a shiny black, chestnut, Pompeian red, white, and leaf gilding. For this composite technique the name *minai* (enamel) is now used by dealers and collectors. Exquisite effects were often obtained by using as ground an opaque glaze stained pale turquoise blue—the colour of a hedge-sparrow's egg, one of the rarest and most surprising in nature. We also find lilac tones and a very deep, resonant blue. Sparing no effort in the cause of enrichment, the potters often built up in relief those parts destined ultimately for gilding: foliage or pierced bosses were worked out in clay applied to the surface before the pot

41

first went to the kiln—sometimes the figures themselves were modelled in high relief (1). Where layer over layer of colour was added, the pot constantly travelling to and fro between the painter and the muffle-kiln, the result became so overwrought as almost to lose the semblance of pottery altogether; one feels that such confections might just as well have been made in plaster of Paris. This is a pity, for the potting is often exquisitely fine, and the shapes, whether demure or frivolous, are mostly appropriate to a ceramic medium. Unfortunately the overglaze colours can be very well imitated by skilful forgers, so that the more obviously expensive *minai* pieces, sometimes furnished with 'interesting' dated inscriptions, are apt to engender more than aesthetic uneasiness.

It appears that the most elaborate *minai* pieces are the earliest; they show big figures, as do the early Persian lustre-wares (2). But very soon the 'miniature' taste already noted in connection with Rayy lustre-ware makes itself felt, and a few pieces were almost certainly decorated by the painters of the Saljuq illuminated manuscripts that have almost all failed to survive the Mongol invasions. Such are the unique dish in M. Kelekian's possession, with a battle scene in which the combatants are labelled by name, as on a Greek vase (3); and the little beaker that presents a series of tableaux from the story of Bizhan in the poet Firdausi's *Shah Nameh* (Book of Kings) (4). Other *Shah Nameh* episodes are occasionally shown, such as the hunting of Bahram Gur and the triumph of Feridun, but the painters usually preferred a purely ornamental arrangement of little horsemen, hunters, and seated princes with their courtiers, all skilfully blended with the more or less intricate arabesques and foliate patterns that sometimes monopolize the field. The 'handwriting' in these little insect-like creatures is of delicious freedom (5). They seem sexless—beards became unartistic early in the thirteenth century, and there are no distinctions between male and female dress. We may notice how the turbans worn by figures on the Fatimid and earlier Rayy lustre pottery have now gone quite out of fashion in favour of Turkish caps.

Rayy, Kashan, and perhaps Sava are places where the *minai* technique was practised, though it has not yet been possible to isolate the different schools with certainty. Rare early experimental pieces show *minai* colours in combination with lustre-painting of the Kashan style. Dates painted on *minai* vessels are often suspect as fraudulent additions, but it seems clear that this exotic kind of pottery sprang up in Persia during the last quarter of the twelfth century and, like the

---

(1) *Plates* 72B, 73B; (2) *Plates* 68A, 69A; (3) *Plate* 70C; (4) *Plate* 70B; (5) *Plate* 74A.

D. *Bowl with 'minai' painting. Persian (perhaps Kashan);
late 12th century. Diam 7¼ in.
Kelekian Collection*

lustre-painted wares of Rayy and Kashan, had passed its best by the time of the Mongol invasions in the 1220's. Some polygonal wall-tiles found at Konia in Asia Minor were probably made there by Persian refugees about 1260. Overglaze colours alone are used in their painting, and this simplification of the technique had apparently become general in Persia by the mid-thirteenth century (1). Abulqasim of Kashan says that in his time (A.D. 1301) the 'seven-colour wares' were no longer made.

But Abulqasim and a later commentator on his work also refer to a *lajvardina* ware still made at the end of the thirteenth century. This can be identified with the pottery and tiles painted over the glaze in a limited palette of opaque red, black, white and gold-leaf, the last being cut into angular shapes before application (2). Glazes of deep rich blue (*lajvard*) and turquoise were favourite ground-colours, and the designs often show the Chinese lotus, phoenix and dragon that became popular under the Ilkhanid Mongol rulers. In shapes the *lajvardina* wares resemble the lustre- and underglaze-painted wares of the Sultanabad district; they tend to be clumsy in potting and uninteresting in ornament. The coarse and greyish body-material is also of inferior quality.

---

(1) *Plates* 72A, 73; (2) *Plates* 74B, 75.

11

UNDERGLAZE PAINTING: EGYPT, MESOPOTAMIA AND PERSIA: TWELFTH-THIRTEENTH CENTURY

The last quarter of the twelfth century saw rapid technical advances in Persia. Painting in lustre and *minai* overglaze colours were then first introduced. A third procedure, that of painting under the alkaline glaze, had been foreshadowed in Persia by the silhouette wares, with designs carried out in thick black slip trimmed with the knife (1). From this it was an easy step to the use of thinner and more tractable underglaze colours that could be painted on by brush.

Egypt. Egyptian potters more quickly realized the possibility than their Persian colleagues. About the time when the Fatimid dynasty fell in 1171, lustre-painting on pottery was superseded by a rather impoverished style of animal-painting in purple monochrome (see p. 24). Very soon the same wiry, prancing animals and birds, with sketchy arabesques and foliage, were being painted in black silhouette under an alkaline glaze either colourless, or stained turquoise, blue or purple. It was then found that firm black outlines could disguise the tendency of cobalt blue to run in the glaze, and a new colour, a dull brownish-red applied as an opaque slip, was sometimes added to complete a severe but very striking triple colour-scheme. The body-material used for these wares of the Ayyubid period in Egypt (1171–1250) was a white paste akin to the Persian but coarser and more granular. Very few pieces survive entire.

Mesopotamia. Both the 'black animal' and the black, blue and red styles of painting soon spread from Egypt to Rakka in Northern Mesopotamia, where, as we have seen, the making of lustre-ware had now begun. It is often very difficult to distinguish between these underglaze-painted wares of Rakka and Egypt: perhaps the Egyptian pieces show finer detail and fewer human figures, and the potting is often thinner than at Rakka. Plates 76–81 illustrate the range of the Rakka painted wares, made probably between about 1171 and the sack of the city by the Mongols in 1259; but the Rakka style was further

---

(1) See p. 35, *Plates* 48–51.

developed and modified at Damascus and perhaps elsewhere in Syria until the fifteenth century. It is claimed that wares of Rakka type were also made at Rusafa, thirty miles distant, but in the absence of kiln-wasters among the finds there this cannot be confirmed. The style has the careless, lashing vigour already noted in the Rakka lustre-ware (p. 38). Hunting and battle scenes are favourite subjects, and the big figures with dotted tree-patterns are more virile relatives of those on the Persian *minai* wares. Here too illuminated manuscripts, of the neighbouring Baghdad school, have probably served as exemplars. Particularly fine are the pieces painted in black under a turquoise glaze. We may notice a *penchant* for big all-over patterns, including a papyrus-like flower not found elsewhere, chequers, and spiral bands. These and the outsize arabesques (1) would seem barbarous to Persian taste. Actually they have much in common with the powerful and austere style found in monuments surviving at Konia in Asia Minor, where the court of the Saljuq rulers of 'Rum' (see p. 29) continued to flourish throughout the time when the Mongols were invading Persia and Mesopotamia. Rakka ware has been found at Konia, and even at Constantinople. Some pieces are painted with the double-headed eagle, the heraldic device of the Saljuqs of Rum that was later adopted by the Austrian Empire.

Persia. Few vessels painted in underglaze colours can be attributed to Rayy, the probable home of the wares ornamented in thick black slip (2). But a bowl painted in black under turquoise glaze (3) is closely associated in style with the Rayy lustre-pottery. At Kashan, however, there was made a whole series of wares painted in black and blue under a colourless or turquoise glaze (4). The blue is either a rich transparent colour apt to run in the glaze, or a pale opaque pigment mixed with some stabilizer—the same pigment that often appears on *minai* ware. Dated pieces range between A.D. 1204 and 1215 There are echoes here of the Kashan lustre style, but new and peculiar arabesque or medallion designs of great delicacy are evolved, and among natural plant-motives the undulating water-weed of Plate 86 is most lovely. The potting is extremely fine, and altogether these Kashan wares are among the most attractive ever made in Persia.

Underglaze painted wares: Sultanabad region. From the evidence of finds it seems that the Kashan manner of underglaze painting, like that of the Kashan lustre-ware, was continued in the second half of the thirteenth century in the region of the modern Sultanabad. From here come clumsier pieces, painted rather tenuously in black under a meagre turquoise glaze (5). Characteristic shapes are narrow-footed

---

(1) *Plate* 80B; (2) See p. 35, *Plates* 48–51; (3) *Plate* 83A; (4) *Plates* 82–89, 92B; (5) *Plates* 90–93.

bowls with external ribbing, and stocky jars, sometimes with multiple handles. A black and green bowl of this class in the Kelekian Collection is dated 677 H/1278 A.D. The glaze of all 'Sultanabad' pottery is very prone to iridescent decay. One small group, made perhaps in a single workshop, is of finer quality (1); most of the pieces are small white bowls or dishes, often ribbed outside and painted with rim-inscriptions in thick white slip. Inside are tiny animals or birds among feathery foliage, crossed inscriptions, or arabesque medallions, almost pen-drawn in greenish black; they are dabbed with green, blue and purple colours that run in the glaze. Two pieces are dated 672/1274 and 729/1329 (2). Wares of this kind may also have been made at Sava and Sultaniyeh.

There is a third type of 'Sultanabad' pottery which has affinities in shape with those already mentioned, but whose decoration marks a departure from the Saljuq tradition. These wares were apparently designed to suit the taste of the Mongol rulers of Persia, of whom Ghazan Khan (1295–1304) was the first to take a constructive interest in Persian art. They and related fourteenth-century wares of Syria and Egypt must be treated in a subsequent volume as representatives of a transitional phase when Islamic pottery had rather lost its sense of direction. Chinese blue-and-white porcelain imported during the fifteenth century eventually supplied the stimulus needed to rescue the art from relapsing into the level of a peasant craft.

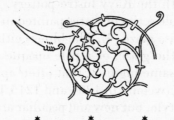

* * * * *

We have reviewed the pottery of Islam during its two greatest epochs; and to judge from the copiousness and variety of wares current at a given time, we must conclude that few civilizations have been so conscious of the potter's art in daily life, from the highest ranks in society to the lowest. It has been barely possible to touch on the important part played by decorated tile-work in Islamic architecture, which belongs mainly to a later period. But on the evidence thus far, what values are absolute in Islamic pottery; and how does it stand in relation to the pottery of other civilizations?

With Ancient Greece and Rome there is sharp contrast. The

---

(1) *Plates* 89B, 90A, 94–6; (2) *Plates* 94, 95A.

techniques of classical Greece were, ceramically speaking, only a refinement of those discovered thousands of years earlier by pre-historic potters. Soft earthenware, painted in earthy pigments of sober colour, without a proper glaze; for even the black colour on Attic pottery is porous, and was fired at too low a heat to fuse. The vitality of the best Greek vases appeals to the intellect rather than the senses. It proceeds from an almost mathematical precision of shape, and from exquisite figure-painting whose first aim is representational rather than decorative. Such painting calls for a flat surface, and is often ill suited to pottery-shapes.

Though in excellent taste, the standard shapes of Islamic pottery were relatively few and simple. There was no seeking after the taut-ness of profile so dear to the Greeks. Gathering up the threads of ancient experience in the Near East, especially from Egypt, mediaeval Islam created a new world of pottery; it was essentially glazed pottery, remarkable for its wealth of colour. Much of this introduction has been devoted to technical comment. It could hardly be otherwise, for at every stage one is aware of the exploring hand on the clay, the active mind devising new means to pass colour and glaze successfully through the ordeal of fire. With Moslem Spain ruled out, contemporary Europe was entirely lacking in such ceramic enterprise, save for a dim flicker round Byzantium. Indeed, European potters since the Renaissance had in their own way to re-tread the same paths. Baghdad potters could make good tin-glazed ware by the ninth century; not till the fifteenth was a comparable ware produced in Christian Europe, where, under the names of maiolica, delft, or faience, it remained our finest form of pottery for over two centuries more. This technique was a direct legacy of Islam, passed on through Moorish Spain. The translucent white Persian wares of the twelfth century anticipated the soft-paste porcelain of France; the overglaze colours of the *minai* technique preceded the enamel colours that appeared in China during the fif-teenth century, and in Europe during the eighteenth. Lustre-painting remained a peculiar glory of Islam, imitated a little in Renaissance Italy, but never attempted in the Far East.

For China, as for the Near East, the early Middle Ages were richly productive. But Chinese potters had a fundamentally different aim. They were preoccupied above all with the substance of their stoneware and porcelain; with its massive hardness and its smoothness of glaze— qualities most readily perceived by the sense of touch. Connoisseurs in the Near East appreciated these values, and, as we have seen, potters tried to reproduce them. But the early tin-glazed imitations of porce-lain could only deceive the eye; and though the Saljuq white wares of the twelfth century are solid, translucent, and agreeable to handle, the artificial paste of most later Islamic pottery has a somewhat harsh and brittle quality. This is unfortunately emphasized by the fragmentary state of surviving pieces and by the decay of their glaze.

The virtues of early Islamic wares are those perceived by the eye. Potters were fascinated by the behaviour of light—light mysteriously refracted by their 'lustre' pigment; light playing over a carved or subtly modelled surface; light gleaming through the glazed 'windows' pierced in the wall of a vessel, or through the translucent material itself. Black-painted ornament swimming under a transparent turquoise glaze is a variant on the same theme. When made opaque with tin-oxide, this turquoise glaze seems to soften and purify the light it absorbs; it has an unearthly beauty, and was considered a charm against evil spirits. All the colours hold something strange to European eyes; a warm glow and subdued intensity very different from the cold brilliance of coloured enamels on Chinese and European porcelain. The ornament, whether painted or carved, almost always springs directly from the ceramic technique; it is rare to find a disproportion between the quality of the medium and the labour spent in its decoration. To the Moslem, a pot was a man-made object of common clay, and perfection was for Allah alone. He might even think it impious to strive after such absolute finish as is found in Chinese porcelain made for the Emperor. The roughness of an unevenly glazed foot-ring is matched by ornament rapidly drawn or carved, without a trace of cramped deliberation. Moslems revere above other arts that of the pen; and Moslem potters worked with the habitual grace of a fluent scribe. We have already spoken in general terms of Islamic ornament and its infinite flexibility to suit a given space. On pottery, as elsewhere, it has a reticent and even elusive quality; it does not force our attention, but detail is there to reward the searching eye. In fact the art of Islam, like that of China, is free from the restless insistence on doctrine or illustration that commonly affects European art; it is at once easy, harmonious and well-bred.

Finally, the early wares of the Near East may remind us of that phase in history when Islam seemed to have inherited the cultural leadership of the mediaeval world. They were made where men were reading Plato, Aristotle, and Galen, in times when most Europeans thought these writers were legendary oriental magicians. The West is once more conscious of its past, and the great cities of the East lie ruined; but we have from them these worn tokens to arouse a sense of vicissitude; and, like the conqueror of Byzantium, we may find it best expressed in the words of Persia's national poet:

The Spider hath wove her web in the Imperial palace;
And the Owl hath sung her watch-song on the towers of Afrasiab.

BIBLIOGRAPHY

Bahgat, A., *La céramique égyptienne de l'époque musulmane* (Cairo, Musée Arabe), 1922.

Bahgat, A. and Massoul, F., *La céramique musulmane de l'Egypte* (Cairo, Musée Arabe), 1930.

Dimand, M. S., *A handbook of Muhammadan art* (Metropolitan Museum, New York), 1944.

Erdmann, K., *Ceramiche di Afrasiab* (In *Faenza* XXV, 1937, 129).

Hobson, R. L., *A guide to the Islamic pottery of the Near East* (British Museum), 1932.

Koechlin, R., *Les céramiques musulmanes de Suse au Musée du Louvre* (Mémoires de la Mission Archéologique de Perse, XIX), 1928.

Kouchakji, F., *Glory of er-Rakka pottery* (In *International Studio*, March, 1923).

Pézard, M., *La céramique archaïque de l'Islam et ses origines*, 1920.

Pope, A. U. (editor), *A survey of Persian art*, 1938.

Rivière, H., *La céramique dans l'art musulman*, 1913.

Ritter, H.; Russka, J.; Sarre, F.; Winderlich, R.; *Orientalische Steinbücher und persische Fayencetechnik*, 1935.

Sarre, F. and Herzfeld, E., *Archäologische Reise im Euphrat- und Tigris-Gebiet*, I (1911); IV (1920).

Sarre, F., *Die Keramik von Samarra* (*Die Ausgrabungen von Samarra* II), 1925.

Ars Islamica, University of Michigan, vol. I, 1934 onwards (articles by various authors).

Bulletin of the Metropolitan Museum of Art, New York; September, 1936; November, 1938; April, 1942 (Reports on Nishapur).

INDEX

INDEX

1. *Blue-green glaze. Syrian or Parthian; about 3rd century A.D. Ht. 12⅝ in. Owner unknown. (page 8)*

2A. *Black painting, turquoise glaze. Egypt, 18th Dynasty; about* 1450
B.C. Diam. 6 in. Eton College. (page 8)
B. *White, purple, green and brown glazes; back turquoise. Egypto-
Roman;* 1st *century B.C. or A.D. Diam.* $8\frac{5}{8}$ *in.
Victoria and Albert Museum. (page* 8)

3. Blue-green glaze. From Susa. Sassanian or early Islamic; 7th–8th century A.D. Ht. 22½ in. Louvre Museum. (page 9)

4A. *Green and yellow lead-glaze. Found at Tyre. Roman: 1st century B.C. or A.D. Ht. 3⅛ in. Kelekian Collection. (page 9)*

B. *Green lead-glaze. Signed 'Husein'. Egypt; 8th–9th century. Berlin State Museum. (page 12)*

C, D. *Unglazed. From Susa. 8th century. Ht. 2¼ in. (cup): Diam. 4½ in. (saucer). Louvre Museum. (page 8)*

E. *Green and yellow lead-glazes. Egypt; 9th century. 6 x 5⅞ in. British Museum. (page 12)*

F. *Green glaze. From Susa. Mesopotamia; 9th century. Diam. 5⅛ in. Louvre Museum. (page 13)*

5A. *Green, brown and purple lead-glazes. Egypt; 8th–9th century.*
Diam. 7¼ in. Formerly Homberg Collection. (page 12)
B. *Relief ornament, gold-lustred lead-glaze. Mesopotamia; 9th*
century. Diam. 10¹³⁄₁₆ in. Charles Vignier. (page 12)

6A. *Unglazed. From Samarra. Mesopotamia; 9th century. Ht. $10\frac{7}{16}$ in. Berlin State Museum. (page 12)*

B. *Lead-glazed sgraffiato ware, mottled green and brown. From Nishapur. Persia; 9th century. Diam. $10\frac{1}{4}$ in. New York, Metropolitan Museum. (page 12)*

7A. *Unglazed, painted yellow, green and purple. From Susa. Mesopotamia; 9th century. Ht. 6½ in. Louvre Museum. (page 12)*
B. *Lead-glazed, mottled green, brown and purple. Perhaps Mesopotamia; 9th century. Diam. 9⅞ in. Sir Alan Barlow. (page 12)*

8. *Mesopotamian tin-glazed wares; painted in blue; 9th century*
A. *Diam. 7⅞ in. Victoria and Albert Museum*
B. *Dish with three feet. Diam. 9⅛ in. Teheran Museum. (page 13)*

9. *Mesopotamian tin-glazed wares; 9th–10th century*
A. *Painted in blue. Signed, 'Made by Salih'. Diam. 8¼ in. De Lorey*
Collection
B. *Painted in blue and green. Diam. 15¼ in. Victoria and Albert*
Museum. (page 13)

10. *Mesopotamian tin-glazed wares, painted in polychrome lustre;*
9th century
A. *Brown and yellow. Diam. 7⅝ in. New York, Metropolitan Museum*
B. *Brown and yellow. Ht. 9¹⁵⁄₁₆ in. Chicago Art Institute (page 15)*

11. *Mesopotamian tin-glazed wares, painted in polychrome lustre;*
9th century

A. *From Susa. Dark brown lustre and opaque yellow-green. Ht. 6½ in.*
Louvre Museum

B. *Brown and yellow. Diam. 8 11/16, Louvre Museum. (page* 15)

12 *Mesopotamian tin-glazed wares, painted in monochrome lustre;*
10th century
A. *Diam.* 7½ *in. Cambridge, Fitzwilliam Museum*
B. *From Rayy. Diam.* 8⅝ *in. Louvre Museum. (page* 16)

13. *Mesopotamian tin-glazed ware, painted in monochrome lustre;*
10th century
A. *From Fostat. Diam. 7⅜ in. Kelekian Collection*
B. *Reverse of a bowl. Berlin State Museum.* (*page 16, 21*)

14. *Slip-painted, purple-black on white. 'Samarkand' wares; 9th–10th century*

A. *'Allah!' From Nishapur. Diam. 9⅝ in. New York, Metropolitan Museum*

B. *'Knowledge: the beginning of it is bitter to taste, but the end is sweeter than honey.' Diam. 14½ in. Louvre Museum. (page 18)*

15. *Slip-painted 'Samarkand' wares; 9th–10th centuries*
A. *Painted in brown-black. Diam.* $9\frac{1}{2}$ *in. Owner unknown*
B. *Painted in brown-black and tomato-red. From Nishapur. Diam. 14*
in. New York, Metropolitan Museum. (page 18)

16. *Slip-painted 'Samarkand' wares; 9th–10th centuries*
A. *Painted in white on purple-black. Diam. 8 in. Victoria and Albert Museum*
B. *Painted in purple-black and tomato-red. From Nishapur. Diam. 10¾ in. New York, Metropolitan Museum. (page 18)*

17. *Slip-painted 'Samarkand' wares; 9th–10th centuries*
A. *Painted in white over brown glaze. Ht. 6⅝ in. Cambridge, Fitz-william Museum*
B. *Painted in yellow-green, with tomato-red and purple touches. Diam. 9½ in. Victoria and Albert Museum. (page 18)*

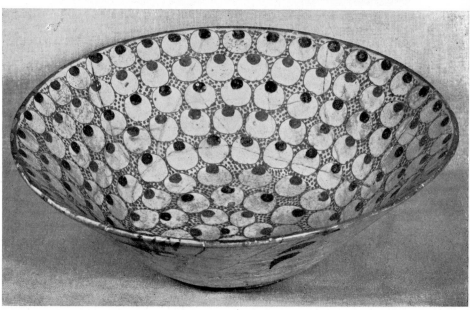

18. *Slip-painted 'Samarkand' bowls; 9th–10th centuries*
A. *Painted in purple-black. From Nishapur. Diam. 10¾ in. New York,*
Metropolitan Museum
B. *Painted in yellow-green, tomato-red, and purple. Diam. 13¹¹⁄₁₆ in.*
British Museum. (page 18)

19. *Slip-painted 'Samarkand' bowls; 9th–10th centuries*
A. *Painted in purple-black. Diam. 10 in. Sir Alan Barlow*
B. *Painted in tomato-red, yellow-green and purple-black. Diam. 9⅞ in.*
Kelekian Collection. (page 18)

20. *Lead-glazed, painted in purple-black, yellow, and green. From Nishapur (Persia)*
A. *Bright yellow ground. 10th century.*
B. *Whitish ground. 9th century. Diam. 8⅛ in. Both, New York, Metropolitan Museum. (page 19)*

21. *Lead-glazed, painted in purple-black and tomato-red slip*
A. *'Samarkand' type; 10th century. Diam. 7¾ in. Victoria and Albert Museum. (page 18)*
B. *Persia (Sari type); 10th–11th century. Diam. 8 in. Kelekian Collection. (page 18)*

22. *Egyptian (Fatimid) wares, painted in lustre*
A. *Signed '(I)brahim in Misr.' Second half of 10th century. Collection*
Aly Pasha Ibrahim
B. *11th century. Cairo, Arab Museum. (pages 21, 22)*

23. *Egyptian (Fatimid) wares, painted in lustre*
A. *Early 11th century*
B. *Early 11th century. Both, Cairo, Arab Museum. (pages 21, 22)*

24. *Egyptian (Fatimid) ware painted in lustre. First half of 12th century. Ht. 12⅜ in. Kelekian Collection. (pages 21, 22)*

25. *Egyptian (Fatimid) wares painted in lustre*
A. *Fragment with name of al-Hakim (996–1021 A.D.)*
B. *11th century. Both, Cairo, Arab Museum. (pages 21, 22)*

26. *Egyptian (Fatimid) wares painted in lustre*
A. *Signed by Saʿd. First half of 12th century. Diam. 8⅝ in. Kelekian*
Collection
B. *12th century. Cairo, Arab Museum. (pages 21, 22)*

27. *Egyptian (Fatimid) wares painted in lustre*
A. *Bowl, built into wall of Church of S. Sisto at Pisa. First half of 12th century*
B. *12th century. Cairo, Arab Museum. (pages 21, 22)*

28. *Egyptian (Fatimid) wares painted in lustre*
A. *Found in Sicily. Middle of 12th century. Diam. 10 in. C. Côte*
Collection, Lyons
B. *Middle of 12th century. Diam.* 5⅛ *in. Kelekian Collection.*
(pages 22, 23)

29. *Egyptian wares*

A. *Painted in lustre on pale turquoise ground. First half of 12th century. Diam. 7⅞ in. Louvre Museum.* (pages 21, 22)

B. *Bowl on high foot, painted in purple under alkaline glaze. Late 12th century. Diam. 5⅜ in. Formerly Martin Collection.* (page 24)

30. *Persian 'sgraffiato' wares*
A. *Green rim. 10th–11th century. Diam. 8⅞ in. Cambridge, Fitz-*
william Museum
B. *10th–11th century. Diam. 13⅝ in. Owner unknown. (page 25)*

31. *Persian 'sgraffiato' and 'champlevé' wares*
A. 10*th*–11*th century. Diam. 7 in. Former Eumorfopoulos Collection*
B. *Garrus district; second half of 12th century. Diam.* 12¼ *in. Victoria
and Albert Museum. (pages 25, 26)*

32. *Persian 'sgraffiato' and 'champlevé' wares*
A. *Incised and painted in green. Amol district; 13th century or later.*
Diam. 8⅞ in. S.A. Lewisohn Collection
B. *Garrus district; 12th–13th century. Ht. 15¼ in. Victoria and Albert*
Museum. (page 27)

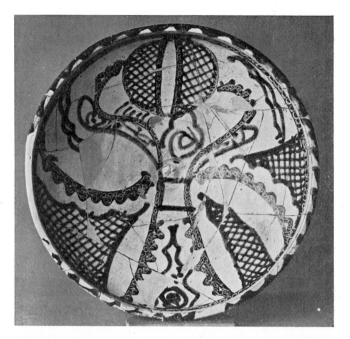

33. Persian 'sgraffiato' and 'champlevé' wares
A. *Incised and painted in brown and green. Amol district; 13th century or later. Diam. 10 in. Victoria and Albert Museum*
B. *Streaked green and purple. Garrus district; second half of 12th–13th century. Diam. 11⅝ in. Kelekian Collection. (page* 27)

34. 'Sgraffiato' wares
A. *Incised and painted in brown and green. Persia, Aghkand district;*
13th century. Diam. 9⅞ in. Owner unknown
B. *Incised and painted in brown and white slip. Egyptian (Mamluk);*
13th–14th century. Diam. 8¼ in. Kelekian Collection. (pages 25, 27)

35. *Syrian 'sgraffiato' wares incised and painted in brown and green;*
13th century
A. *Diam. 11⅛ in. Washington, Freer Gallery*
B. *Found near Aleppo. Diam. 10⅕ in. British Museum. (page 26)*

36. *Unglazed pottery*

A. *Moulded ornament. ? Mesopotamia; 11th–12th century. Ht. 6½ in.*
British Museum

B. *Impressed ornament. Mesopotamia or Persia; 12th–13th century*
Ht. 4⅝ in. Victoria and Albert Museum

C. *Moulded ornament. From Al Mina near Antioch. Syria; 9th–10th*
century. Ht. 7¼ in. Victoria and Albert Museum

D, E. *Filters from necks of jugs. From Fostat. Egypt; 11th–13th*
century? Victoria and Albert and Cairo Museums

F. *Moulded, green-glazed. From Rakka. 12th–13th century? Ht. 4⅝ in.*
Victoria and Albert Museum. (page 27)

57. *Unglazed pottery*

A. *Found near Aleppo. Syria; 13th–14th century. Ht. 11⅛ in. Victoria and Albert Museum*

B. *Top of large jar. Mesopotamia; second half of 12th or 13th century. Ht. 12¾ in. Victoria and Albert Museum. (page 28)*

38. *Carved white Saljuq pottery from Persia. First half of* 12*th century*
A. *Ht.* $4\frac{3}{8}$ *in. Victoria and Albert Museum*
B. *Diam.* $7\frac{3}{4}$ *in. Victoria and Albert Museum*
C. *Diam.* $7\frac{1}{4}$ *in. Sir Alan Barlow.* (*page* 33)

39. *Carved white Saljuq pottery from Persia. Mainly first half of*
12th century
A. *Ht. 4½ in. Victoria and Albert Museum*
B. *Glaze-filled piercing, incised decoration, and blue rim. Ht. 5⅝ in.*
Victoria and Albert Museum
C. *Diam. 6½ in. Victoria and Albert Museum*
D. *Diam. 8½ in. Hague Museum. (page 33)*

40. *Carved wares with monochrome glazes*

A. *Turquoise-blue with pierced transparencies. Persia; second half of*
12th century. Diam. 7$\frac{1}{16}$ in. Teheran Museum

B. *White, green, polychrome, and brown. From Fostat. Egypt; 12th–*
13th century. Victoria and Albert Museum. (pages 23, 34, 35)

41. *Carved Saljuq bowls from Persia, with blue glaze. Mid-12th century*
A. *Diam. 7¼ in. Victoria and Albert Museum*
B. *Diam. 10¹⁄₁₆ in. Sir Alan Barlow. (page 34)*

42. *Carved and moulded Persian wares with monochrome glazes*
A. *Moulded, opaque turquoise glaze. Second half of 12th century Ht.* $5\frac{1}{8}$ *in. British Museum*
B. *Moulded and carved, deep blue glaze. Late 12th century. Ht.* $4\frac{3}{4}$ *in. Bois Collection*
C. *Moulded, dark blue glaze. From near Sultanabad; second half of 13th century. Ht.* $11\frac{3}{8}$ *in. Kelekian Collection*
D. *Moulded, dark blue glaze. 13th century. Ht. 9 in. Berlin State Museum. (page 34)*

43.*Carved wares with turquoise glaze. Persia (? Rayy). Second half of 12th century*
A. *Diam.* $7\frac{1}{16}$ *in. Teheran Museum*
B. *Ht.* $6\frac{5}{16}$ *in. Victoria and Albert Museum*
C. *Red outlines and gilding added over the glaze. Diam.* $15\frac{3}{8}$ *in. Sir Alan Barlow. (page 34)*

44. *Carved, with opaque turquoise glaze. Persia; 12th–13th century*
Ht. 31½ in. New York, Metropolitan Museum. (page 34)

45. *Carved or moulded ware with turquoise glaze. Mesopotamia*
(Rakka). 12th–13th century
A. *Lamp. Ht. 7⅞ in. Owner unknown*
B. *Floor-table. Owner unknown.* (*page 34*)

46. 'Lakabi' carved dishes with polychrome glazes. Persia; mid-12th
century
A. *Diam. 8⅝ in. Owner unknown*
B. *Diam. 11⅞ in. New York, Metropolitan Museum. (page 35)*

47. 'Lakabi' carved wares with polychrome glazes. Persia; mid-12th
century
A. *Ht. 5⅝in. Victoria and Albert Museum*
B. *Ht. 7¼ in. Owner unknown*
C. *Diam. 16⅛ in. Berlin State Museum. (page 35)*

48. *Black slip silhouette under clear ivory glaze. Persia; second half of 12th century. Diam. 8⅛ in. Ht. 3⅛ in. Sir Alan Barlow. (pages 35, 36)*

49. *Black slip silhouette under clear glaze. Persia; second half of*
12th century
A. *Turquoise glaze. Diam. 8⅝ in. Sir Alan Barlow*
B. *Clear ivory glaze. Diam. 7⅛ in. Kelekian Collection. (pages 35, 36)*

50. *Black slip silhouette under clear turquoise glaze. Persia; second
half of 12th century*
A. *Diam.* $7\frac{1}{8}$ *in. Cambridge, Fitzwilliam Collection*
B. *Money-bowl. Diam.* $6\frac{3}{4}$ *in. Ht.* $3\frac{3}{8}$ *in. Victoria and Albert Museum.*
(pages 35, 36)

51. *Black slip silhouette under clear turquoise glaze. Persia; second half of 12th century*

A. *Diam. 7¼ in. Victoria and Albert Museum*

B. *Sir Alan Barlow*

C. *Ht. 5 in. Victoria and Albert Museum.* (*pages* 35, 36)

52. *Lustre-painted wares. Persia (Rayy); late 12th century*
A. *Ht. 7¾ in. Godman Collection*
B. *Dated 575/1179 A.D. Ht. 5½ in. British Museum*
C. *Diam. 14¼ in. Victoria and Albert Museum. (pages 37, 38)*

53. *Lustre-painted wares. Persia (Rayy); late 12th–early 13th century*
A. *Vase in form of woman and child. Berlin State Museum*
B. *Ht. 7 in. Washington, Freer Gallery*
C. *Diam. 14 in. New York, Metropolitan Museum. (pages 37 ,38)*

54. *Lustre-painted wares. Persia (Rayy); late 12th century*
A. *Ht. 7⅜ in. Victoria and Albert Museum*
B. *Diam. 8⅝ in. Kelekian Collection*
C. *Diam. 11 3/16 in. Berlin State Museum. (pages 37, 38)*

55. *Lustre-painted wares. Persia (Rayy); late 12th century*
A. *Diam.* $9\frac{1}{16}$ *in. Berlin State Museum*
B. *Painted on deep blue glaze. Ht.* $8\frac{1}{2}$ *in. Formerly Eumorfopoulos Collection*
C. *Dated* 587/1191 *A.D. Diam.* $14\frac{15}{16}$ *in. Boston Museum. (pages* 37, 38)

56. *Lustre-painted wares. Persia (Rayy); late 12th–early 13th century*
A. *Ht. 5¾ in. Victoria and Albert Museum*
B. *Ht. 13¼ in. Godman Collection*
C. *Ht. 10 in Kelekian Collection. (pages 37, 38)*

57. *Lustre-painted wares. Mesopotamia (Rakka); late 12th or first half
of 13th century.*
A. *Ht. 9½ in. Kelekian Collection.*
B. *Diam. about 14 in. Walters Art Gallery, Baltimore. (pages 38, 39)*

58. *Lustre-painted wares. Persia (Rayy)*
A. *First half 13th century. Diam. 13⅞ in. Victoria and Albert Museum*
B. *Late 12th century. Diam. 16¾ in. New York, Metropolitan Museum.*
(*pages 37, 38*)

59. *Lustre-painted wares. Mesopotamia (Rakka) late 12th–first half of*
13th century
A. *Diam.* 14¼ *in. Cleveland Museum, Ohio*
B. *Diam.* 11½ *in. Kelekian Collection. (pages 38, 39)*

60. *Carved, with painting in lustre and blue. Mesopotamia (Rakka);*
late 12th–first half of 13th century
A. *Ht. 17 in. Godman Collection*
B. *Floor-table. Width 11⅕ in. British Museum. (pages 38, 39)*

61. *Painted in lustre. Persian (Kashan); early 13th century. Ht. 27 in.*
Hirsch Collection (pages 39, 40)

62. *Lustre-painted wares. Persia (Kashan); early* 13*th century*
A. *Dated* 604/1207 *A.D. Diam.* 13¾ *in. Kelekian Collection*
B. *Detail from a large dish; bridal procession. Kelekian Collection*
(*pages* 39, 40)

63. *Lustre-painted wares. Persia (Kashan); early 13th century*
A. *Dated 607/1210 A.D. Diam. 11¾ in. New York, Metropolitan Museum*
B. *Floor-table. Ht. 10¼ in. McIlhenny Collection. (pages 39, 40)*

64. *Persian wares painted in lustre*

A. *Sultanabad district; early 14th century. Diam.* 8½ *in. Victoria and Albert Museum*

B. *Kashan; dated 607/1210 A.D. Diam.* 13⅜ *in. Formerly Eumor-fopoulos Collection.* (*pages* 39, 40)

65. *Persian wares painted in lustre*

A. *Sultanabad district; 13th century. Ht. $9\frac{7}{16}$ in. Kelekian Collection*

B. *Kashan or Sultanabad district; dated 668/1269 A.D. Diam. $7\frac{1}{16}$ in. Kelekian Collection*

C. *Sultanabad district; early 14th century. Diam. $7\frac{1}{8}$ in. Owner unknown. (page 40)*

66. *Lustre and blue-painted 'mihrab' (prayer-niche) from the Maydan Mosque at Kashan. Signed by Hasan ibn-Arabshah al-Nakkash. Persia (Kashan); dated 623/1226 A.D. Berlin State Museum.*
(*pages* 39, 40)

67. *Persian (Kashan) lustre-painted wall-tiles*

A. *From border of a 'mihrab'. Raised lettering in blue. Signed by Hasan ibn-Arabshah al-Nakkash; about 1225. Ht. 18½ in. Victoria and Albert Museum*

B. *Lower star-tiles from a series at Damghan dated 665–6/1266–7 A.D.; upper star with camel dated 1289. Berlin State Museum.*

(*pages* 39, 40)

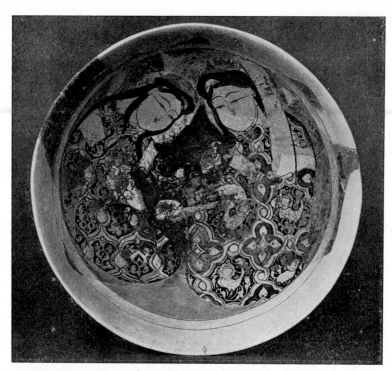

68. *Polychrome 'minai' painted bowls. Persian; late 12th or early 13th*
century
A. *Diam. 8¼ in. Kelekian Collection*
B. *Diam. 8⅛ in. Victoria and Albert Museum. (page 42)*

69. *Polychrome 'minai' painted bowls. Persian; late 12th or early*
13th century
A. *Diam. 9½ in. Kelekian Collection*
B. *Diam. 8⅜ in. Victoria and Albert Museum. (page 42)*

70. *Polychrome 'minai' painted wares. Persian; late 12th or first half of 13th century*
A. *Posset-pot. Ht. 6½ in. British Museum*
B. *Scenes from the 'Shah-Nameh'. Ht. 4⅜ in. Washington, Freer Gallery*
C. *Expedition of a Saljuq emir. Diam. 18¹¹⁄₁₆ in. Kelekian Collection.*
(*page 42*)

71. *Polychrome 'minai' and overglaze painted wares. Late 12th or
first half of 13th century*
A. *Diam.* 8⅛ *in. Kelekian Collection*
B. *Ht.* 8 1/10 *in. Owner unknown*
C. *Overglaze painting, gilt bosses, opaque turquoise ground. Ht.* 10⅞ *in.
Kelekian Collection. (pages 42, 43)*

72. *Polychrome 'minai' and overglaze-painted wares. Persian; mid-13th century*

A. *Opaque turquoise ground. Dated 640/1242 A.D. Diam. 7¾ in.*
Victoria and Albert Museum

B. *Wall-tile, moulded in relief, opaque turquoise ground. 7⅞ in. square*
Paravicini Collection. (page 43)

73. *Persian polychrome overglaze-painted wares*
A. *Mid-13th century. Diam.* $9\frac{7}{16}$ *in. Owner unknown*
B. *Moulded in relief. Opaque turquoise ground. Mid-13th century*
Diam. $11\frac{3}{8}$ *in. Sir Ernest Debenham. (page* 43)

74. *Persian overglaze-painted wares*
A. *Fragment of a 'minai' painted bowl. Early 13th century. Gerald Reitlinger Collection*
B. *Opaque turquoise ground. Mid-13th century. Diam. 13¾ in. Louvre Museum. (pages 42, 43)*

75. *Persian overglaze-painted (lajvardina) wares. About* 1300 *A.D.*
A. *Deep blue ground. Diam.* 6⅛ *in. Victoria and Albert Museum*
B. *Wall-tiles. Alternately deep blue and opaque turquoise ground. Diam.*
of stars 5 *in. Victoria and Albert Museum.* (*page* 43)

76. *Black painting under clear turquoise glaze*
Mesopotamia (Rakka); late 12th or first half 13th century. Ht. 10½ in.
Victoria and Albert Museum. (pages 44, 45)

77. *Black painting under clear glaze. Mesopotamia (Rakka); late 12th–*
first half 13th century
A. *Colourless glaze. Ht.* 6⅝ *in. Victoria and Albert Museum*
B. *Turquoise glaze. Diam.* 11⅛ *in. New York, Metropolitan Museum.*
(pages 44, 45)

78. *Painted in underglaze black, blue, and brown-red. Mesopotamia
(Rakka); late 12th–first half 13th century*
A. *Diam.* 9½ *in. Berlin State Museum*
B. *Diam.* 10¼ *in. Victoria and Albert Museum. (pages 44, 45)*

79. *Painted in underglaze black, blue, and brown-red. Mesopotamia*
(Rakka); late 12th–first half 13th century
A. *Diam.* 8½ *in. British Museum*
B. *Diam.* 10¾ *in. Victoria and Albert Museum. (pages 44, 45)*

80. *Painted in black under clear glaze. Mesopotamia (Rakka); late
12th–first half 13th century*
A. *Colourless glaze. Ht. about 11 in. Owner unknown*
B. *Turquoise glaze. Diam. $10\frac{1}{10}$ in. Victoria and Albert Museum.*
(*pages* 44, 45)

81. *Painted in underglaze black and blue. Mesopotamia (Rakka); late*
12th–first half 13th century
A. *Diam. 9⅝ in. Victoria and Albert Museum*
B. *Diam. 11¹³⁄₁₆ in. New York, Metropolitan Museum. (pages 44, 45)*

82. *Painted in black under turquoise glaze*
Persia (Kashan); early 13th century. Ht. 14¾ in. Cambridge,
Fitzwilliam Museum (page 45)

83. Painted in black under clear glazes

A. *Turquoise glaze. Rayy; early 13th century. Diam. 8 in. Kelekian
Collection*

B. *Turquoise glaze, blue streaks. Pierced outer shell. Kashan; dated
612/1215 A.D. Ht. 7¾ in. New York, Metropolitan Museum*
(page 45)

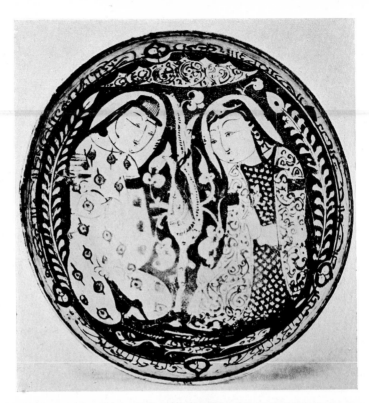

84. *Painted in underglaze black and blue. Persia (Kashan); early 13th century*

A. *Diam.* 7⅞ *in. Owner unknown*

B. *Dated* 610H/1214 *A.D. Diam. 8 in. Sir Ernest Debenham*

(*page* 45)

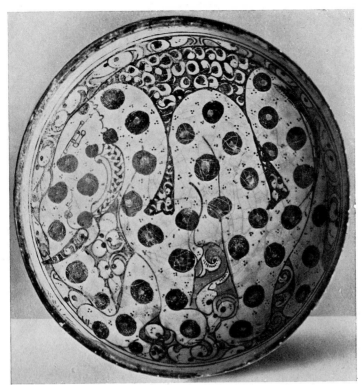

85. *Painted in underglaze black and blue. Persia (Kashan); early 13th century*
A. *Diam. 7¾ in. Victoria and Albert Museum*
B. *Diam. 8⅛ in. Victoria and Albert Museum. (page 45)*

86. *Bowl painted in underglaze black; pale blue inner rim. Persia (Kashan); early 13th century. Diam. 7¾ in. Ht. 4¼ in. Victoria and Albert Museum. (page 45)*

87. *Painted in underglaze black and pale blue. Persia (Kashan); early*
13th century
A. *Diam. 8⅛ in.*
B. *Diam. 8 in. Both, Victoria and Albert Museum. (page 45)*

88. *Decorated in relief and in black painting under turquoise glaze Persia (Kashan); early 13th century. Ht. 12¾ in. R. Armsby Collection. (page 45)*

89. *Persian wares painted in underglaze black and blue, with pierced transparencies*
A. *Kashan; early 13th century. Ht. 4¾ in. Victoria and Albert Museum*
B. *From Sultanabad; late 13th century. Diam. 7⅝ in. Kelekian Collection.* (*pages* 45, 46)

90. *Underglaze painted wares. Persian (Kashan or Sultanabad district)*
13th century
A. *Blue stripes. Ht.* 4¼ *in. Victoria and Albert Museum*
B. *Black under turquoise glaze. Diam.* 10¼ *in. Sir Ernest Debenham*
(pages 45, 46)

91. *Painted in black under turquoise glaze. Persian (Sultanabad district); second half of 13th century. Ht. 11⅜ in. Victoria and Albert Museum. (pages 45, 46)*

92. *Persian wares painted in black under turquoise glaze*

A. *Sultanabad district; second half of 13th century. Ht. $9\frac{1}{2}$ in. Kelekian Collection*

B. *Black and blue under turquoise. Kashan; early 13th century. Ht. $3\frac{7}{8}$ in. Diam. $8\frac{7}{8}$ in. Sir Alan Barlow. (pages 45, 46)*

93. *Bowl, painted in black under turquoise glaze. Persia (Sultanabad district); second half of 13th century. Diam.* 8⅝ *in. Ht.* 4¼ *in. Kelekian Collection. (pages 45, 46)*

94. *Bowl painted in underglaze green-black, blue, green, and purple Persia (Sultanabad district); dated 672/1274 A.D. Diam. 7 in. Ht. 4½ in. Kelekian Collection. (page 46)*

95. *Painted in underglaze green-black, blue, green and purple. Persia*
(*Sultanabad district*)
A. *Dated 729H/1329 A.D. Royal Ontario Museum of Archaeology*
B. *Late 13th century. Cambridge, Fitzwilliam Museum* (*page 46*)

96. *Bowls painted in underglaze green-black, blue, green and purple.*
Persia (Sultanabad district); late 13th century.
A. *Diam.* 4½ *in.*
B. *Diam.* 6 *in. Both, Victoria and Albert Museum. (page* 46)